Win in Chinese Courts

Chenyang Zhang

Win in Chinese Courts

Practice Guide to Civil Litigation in China

 Springer

Chenyang Zhang
China Life Finance Centre
Beijing, China

Beijing Tian Yuan Law Firm
Beijing, China

ISBN 978-981-99-3341-9   ISBN 978-981-99-3342-6 (eBook)
https://doi.org/10.1007/978-981-99-3342-6

© The Editor(s) (if applicable) and The Author(s) 2023. This book is an open access publication.

Open Access This book is licensed under the terms of the Creative Commons Attribution 4.0 International License (http://creativecommons.org/licenses/by/4.0/), which permits use, sharing, adaptation, distribution and reproduction in any medium or format, as long as you give appropriate credit to the original author(s) and the source, provide a link to the Creative Commons license and indicate if changes were made.

The images or other third party material in this book are included in the book's Creative Commons license, unless indicated otherwise in a credit line to the material. If material is not included in the book's Creative Commons license and your intended use is not permitted by statutory regulation or exceeds the permitted use, you will need to obtain permission directly from the copyright holder.

The use of general descriptive names, registered names, trademarks, service marks, etc. in this publication does not imply, even in the absence of a specific statement, that such names are exempt from the relevant protective laws and regulations and therefore free for general use.

The publisher, the authors, and the editors are safe to assume that the advice and information in this book are believed to be true and accurate at the date of publication. Neither the publisher nor the authors or the editors give a warranty, expressed or implied, with respect to the material contained herein or for any errors or omissions that may have been made. The publisher remains neutral with regard to jurisdictional claims in published maps and institutional affiliations.

This Springer imprint is published by the registered company Springer Nature Singapore Pte Ltd.
The registered company address is: 152 Beach Road, #21-01/04 Gateway East, Singapore 189721, Singapore

Foreword

As an Australian lawyer with over 30 years of experience specializing in insolvency and dispute resolution, it is becoming increasingly more common, in the current economic downturn, for me to see disputes with Chinese investors in local ventures, particularly in real estate, mining and infrastructure sectors. Although cross-border insolvency laws and enforcement are fairly well developed and understood in Australia, there is much uncertainty when such laws interact with investment agreements governed by Chinese local law and its civil litigation or CIETAC arbitration systems. As liquidators and other insolvency appointees representing the interests of third-party creditors, they usually are looking for certainly and the most fair, efficient and timely determination of those claims to secure the best or highest return. For this reason, Australian insolvency practitioners have traditionally avoided the mysterious and unfamiliar Chinese dispute resolution system instead preferring to have such claims determined by their local proof of debt and other insolvency procedures and forcing foreign creditors to submit to those laws.

However, in a recent large Australian mining investment dispute, our liquidator client was dragged into CIETAC by Chinese state-owned investors following the making of the first emergency order which restrained the liquidator from making any distributions, except to priority employee claims, pending a final CIETAC determination. In this matter, I had the pleasure of working with Chenyang in successfully resisting those proceedings and subsequent attempts to appeal the CIETAC determination on the public policy grounds of alleged fraud.

Chenyang was able to alleviate the liquidator's concerns by his commercial and common-sense approach by throwing light on the Chinese dispute resolution system. One of Chenyang's strengths is his ability to translate into English and explain the differences in meaning, terminology and legal system. That was particularly critical in our dispute which concerned the interpretation of specific wording in a Chinese investment agreement and how CIETAC arbitrators weighed different kinds of evidence. It was particularly surprising that even in a civil contractual dispute between two investing parties, how much weight is given to the agreement itself, while investigations and studies with little or no credence being given to oral statement from the interested contracting parties themselves which was not treated as a kind of evidence at all. As far as I can see, arbitrations in different jurisdictions share common features in many aspects, but such experience showed how important it is to distinguish and understand those differences.

Based on such experience, I am quite curious about the civil litigation in China which has so many differences from those in Australia and many other countries, and a concise and straightforward handbook written by my Chinese counterparts will be of great help as I can foresee. This practical guide is exactly what I expect. It will serve as a valuable tool for foreign lawyers and practitioners in enlightening them to the Chinese dispute resolution system and assist in alleviating any perceptions as its fairness and efficiencies. I believe this guide will be helpful to its readers, especially those who need to know the Chinese civil litigation in short time and easy ways.

Philip Pan
Partner at King and Wood Mallesons
Brisbane, Australia

Preface

With China's continuous expansion of its opening-up policy, more foreign investments and trades are being attracted to China, and the foreign-related cases filed by Chinese courts are increasing dramatically. From 2016 to September 2021, more than 330,000 commercial and maritime cases with foreign-related elements were heard and closed by courts in China, and the number of other foreign-related civil cases (including intellectual property cases) is quite big as well. In addition, the enforcement of court judgment in China, including tracking and recovering properties of the losing party, is becoming more and more impressive and effective with the help of online information system. Therefore, filing a case in China is both a good option for the plaintiff and a serious alert for the defendant.

However, as a Chinese lawyer specializing in cross-border dispute resolution for more than ten years, I become aware of the fact that the civil litigation system in China is still quite mysterious and unfamiliar to many foreign lawyers. Some people even call it a "black box" and advise others to avoid participating in litigation in China, either actively or passively.

In fact, China has developed a mature and full-scale civil litigation system with sophisticated statutes and provisions, which can effectively support foreign parties to resolve dispute in China. Unfortunately, such information is often neglected by my counterparts due to lack of systematic summary and necessary interpretation, and many disputes resolvable in China remain unsettled for a long time.

To fill such information gap, this guide tries to present a comprehensive roadmap of civil litigation system in China. It will start from some basic concepts of Chinese judicial system (such as the court system, case numbering, hierarchical trial system) and go through the whole process and most aspects of a civil litigation case (such as jurisdiction, case filing, service of court documents, evidence rules, process of trial, enforcement of judgments and court costs).

With titles in form of questions or containing key elements of corresponding sections, I understand this guide to be a "dictionary" to easily learn about specific topics of civil litigation in China. Or else, it can also serve as a highly simplified and condensed textbook to learn about civil litigation in China in less than half a day. I hope this guide can answer the most frequently asked questions from legal practitioners, scholars, students and others who are interested in civil litigation in China.

To avoid misunderstanding, here are some notes for readers. The term "China" in this guide, unless otherwise defined, refers to Mainland China and does not include Hong Kong Special Administrative Region, Macau Special Administrative Region and Taiwan region. This guide does not discuss criminal or administrative litigation in China, and "civil" litigation in this guide includes commercial litigation and intellectual property litigation. Although maritime litigation is categorized as civil litigation in China, it cannot be fully covered by this guide due to its particularity in procedures. This guide is prepared based on laws, judicial interpretations, other provisions and information effective as of December 2022, which may be updated from time to time. The reference provisions enumerated in the end of each section are those closely related to the section, rather than a complete list of all relevant provisions. Some contents are prepared based on personal or peer experience, rather than official or authoritative literatures. This guide does not constitute any legal opinion or service to any person. Given my personal experience and ability are limited, mistakes and inaccuracies are unavoidable in this guide. If you find them, please feel free to contact me and I am more than happy to correct them.

At last, I would like to thank Ms. Meng Yu and Mr. Guodong Du, who have strongly encouraged me to write this guide and shared many of their brilliant ideas and helpful comments. I would also like to thank Mr. Haibin Lin, who has made great efforts to polish the writing of this guide. Their help and contribution are indispensable for the publication of this guide. Finally, please allow me to express my gratitude to Springer, my family, and those supporting me as always.

That is all. Hope you find this guide useful and enjoy reading it.

Beijing, China   Chenyang Zhang

Contents

1	**Some Basic Concepts and Systems**		1
	1.1 China's Court System—Magnificent 4-Level Pyramid		1
		1.1.1 The 4-Level System of Chinese Courts	1
		1.1.2 The Classification of Chinese Courts	2
		1.1.3 Separate Functions of Courts at All Levels	4
	1.2 China's Hierarchical Trial System for Civil Cases—2 + 1 + 1		5
		1.2.1 Most Cases Are Closed After the Second Instance	5
		1.2.2 Simple and Small Claim Cases Are Closed After the First Instance	6
		1.2.3 After the Final Trial of a Case, the Parties May also Apply for Retrial	7
		1.2.4 After the Application for Retrial Is Dismissed, the Parties May also Apply to the Procuratorate for Case Review	7
		1.2.5 After the End of the "2 + 1 + 1" Procedure, the Parties May Still Be Entitled to Petition in Theory	8
		1.2.6 Cases that Are not Subject to the "2 + 1 + 1" Procedure	8
	1.3 Case Numbering System of Chinese Courts—"Secret Signal" in Case Number		9
		1.3.1 Basic Format of Case Number	9
		1.3.2 Compilation Rules for Court Codes	9
		1.3.3 Compilation Rules for Case Type Codes	11
	1.4 Cause of Action—Index List of Chinese Case Classification		13
		1.4.1 The Development of Cause of Action in Civil Cases	13
		1.4.2 How to Determine the Cause of Action in the Case	14
		1.4.3 Functions of the Cause of Action	15
	1.5 How Do Chinese Courts Charge—Court Costs		17
		1.5.1 Fee Rates of Chinese Courts	17

		1.5.2	Special Circumstances of Fee Reduction/ Exemption	18
		1.5.3	Payment Time and Method	19
		1.5.4	The Court Costs Shall Be Borne by the Losing Party	19
	1.6	General Process of Civil Litigation in China		20
	1.7	Chinese Lawyers in Civil Litigation		20
		1.7.1	Formulating Evidence Presentation Strategies Is One of the Core Tasks of Chinese Lawyers	21
		1.7.2	Chinese Lawyers Can Investigate and Collect Evidence on the Strength of a Court Investigation Order	21
		1.7.3	Confidentiality Obligations of Chinese Lawyers	22
		1.7.4	Charging Modes of Chinese Lawyers	23
2	**Jurisdiction**			**25**
	2.1	Which Level of Court Does My Case Go to—Hierarchical Jurisdiction System		26
		2.1.1	How to Determine the Hierarchical Jurisdiction	26
		2.1.2	No Change of the Level of a Competent Court by Agreement and Its Exceptions	27
		2.1.3	Elevated Jurisdiction and Delegated Jurisdiction	27
	2.2	The Court of Which Place Has Jurisdiction—Territorial Jurisdiction System		29
		2.2.1	Respect the Agreement Reached by the Parties	29
		2.2.2	The Place Where the Defendant Is Located: Connecting Factor for Most Cases	30
		2.2.3	The Place Where the Contract Is Performed: Connecting Factor for Contract Disputes	30
		2.2.4	The Place Where the Infringement Is Committed and the Infringement Result Occurs: Connecting Factors for Infringement Disputes	31
		2.2.5	The Place Where the Company Is Domiciled: Connecting Factor for Company-Related Organic Disputes	32
		2.2.6	Prorogated Jurisdiction Rules	32
		2.2.7	Exclusive Jurisdiction Rules	33
		2.2.8	Cross-Region Centralized Jurisdiction of Specific Cases	33
		2.2.9	Special Rules in Case of Foreign Parties as Defendants	34
	2.3	Objection to Jurisdiction and Case Transferring		35
		2.3.1	The Defendant May Raise an Objection to Jurisdiction	35

| | | 2.3.2 | The Court May also Examine the Jurisdiction Issue Ex Officio | 36 |
| | | 2.3.3 | Case Transferring | 36 |

3 Case Filing and Determination of the Adjudicatory Personnel 39
   3.1 Preparations Before Bringing a Lawsuit—Formality Documents for Foreign Parties 39
      3.1.1 Certificates of Subject Qualification—"Who Am I" and "Who Represents Me" 39
      3.1.2 Power of Attorney—"Who Is My Lawyer" 40
      3.1.3 Notarization and Authentication—"My Documents Are Authentic" 41
      3.1.4 Translation 43
   3.2 Bringing a Lawsuit and Case Filing 43
      3.2.1 General Process of Case Filing 43
      3.2.2 Cross-Border Online Case Filing—Latest Facilitation Measures for Foreign Parties 44
   3.3 Determining the Adjudicatory Personnel 46
      3.3.1 The Composition of Collegial Panel 46
      3.3.2 No Jury in China—What Is People's Assessor 47

4 Service of Court Documents 51
   4.1 Basic Methods for Service of Court Documents in China 52
      4.1.1 Personal Service 52
      4.1.2 Service by Leaving Rejected Court Documents at the Domicile 52
      4.1.3 Service by Mail 52
      4.1.4 Electronic Service 53
      4.1.5 Service by Publication 53
   4.2 How to Tackle "Difficulty in Effecting Service of Court Documents" 54
      4.2.1 Reform Measures for "Difficulty in Effecting Service of Court Documents" on Enterprises 54
      4.2.2 Vigorously Promote Electronic Service 54
      4.2.3 Combat Service Evasion 54
   4.3 How to Serve Court Documents on Foreign Parties Without Domicile in China 56
      4.3.1 Service on Personnel or Organizations in China 56
      4.3.2 Service Under the Hague Service Convention and Other International Treaties 57
      4.3.3 Service Through Diplomatic Channels 57
      4.3.4 Service by Mail 57
      4.3.5 Electronic Service 58
      4.3.6 Service by Publication 58
   4.4 How Do Chinese Courts Assist Foreign Courts in Service of Court Documents 59

		4.4.1	Assistance in Service Under the Hague Service Convention	59
		4.4.2	Assistance in Service Under Bilateral Treaties	60
5	**Trial**			63
	5.1	Pretrial Preparations		64
		5.1.1	Defense and Presentation of Evidence	64
		5.1.2	Exchange of Evidence and Pretrial Conference	65
	5.2	Court Hearing		66
		5.2.1	Court-Conducted Investigation	66
		5.2.2	Debates in Court	66
		5.2.3	Closing Argument	67
		5.2.4	Mediation	67
		5.2.5	Noteworthy Points in Court Hearing	67
	5.3	First-Instance Judgment		69
	5.4	Second-Instance Procedure		69
	5.5	Time Limit for Trial		70
	5.6	Summary Procedure		71
		5.6.1	What Is Summary Procedure?	71
		5.6.2	Difference Between Summary Procedure and Ordinary Procedure	72
	5.7	Small Claims Procedure—A Further Simplified Summary Procedure		73
	5.8	Foreign-Related Cases—Special Rules for Foreign Parties' Participation in China's Litigation		74
		5.8.1	What Are Foreign-Related Cases?	74
		5.8.2	What Is Special About Foreign-Related Cases?	74
		5.8.3	Prohibition on Submitting Non-Foreign-Related Cases to Foreign Courts or Arbitration Institutions	75
6	**Evidence**			77
	6.1	Standard of Proof		77
		6.1.1	Most To-Be-Proved Facts Subject to "Preponderance of the Evidence" Standard	78
		6.1.2	Special To-Be-Proved Facts Subject to "Beyond a Reasonable Doubt" Standard	78
	6.2	Burden of Proof		79
		6.2.1	What Is Burden of Proof	79
		6.2.2	Core of the Rule—The Burden of Proof Lies with the Party Asserting a Proposition	79
		6.2.3	The Shift in the Burden of Proof	80
		6.2.4	The Reversal of the Burden of Proof	80
	6.3	Time Limit for Presenting Evidence		81
		6.3.1	What Is Time Limit for Presenting Evidence	82

		6.3.2	How to Determine the Time Limit for Presenting Evidence	82
		6.3.3	Legal Consequences of Late Evidence Presentation	82
		6.3.4	How to Deal with Surprise Evidence	83
	6.4	Self-admission System		84
		6.4.1	What Adverse Statement Would Constitute Self-admission?	84
		6.4.2	The Legal Effect of Self-admission	85
		6.4.3	Some Special Circumstances	85
	6.5	Witness Testimony		87
		6.5.1	Who Can Be a Witness	87
		6.5.2	How to Apply for a Witness to Testify in Court	87
		6.5.3	Can a Witness Be Spared Appearing in Court	88
		6.5.4	Does China Have a Cross-Examination System	88
		6.5.5	Who Will Bear the Cost of the Witness Testimony	88
		6.5.6	What Is the Effect of Witness Testimony in Practice	89
		6.5.7	Conclusions and Suggestions	89
	6.6	Expert Witness in China?—Expert Assistant		90
		6.6.1	What Is Expert Assistant?	90
		6.6.2	Who Can Be the Expert Assistant?	91
		6.6.3	How to Apply for the Expert Assistant to Appear in Court?	91
		6.6.4	What Issues Can the Expert Assistant Express Opinions On?	92
		6.6.5	The Effectiveness of the Expert Assistant Opinions in Practice	92
		6.6.6	Conclusion	93
	6.7	Can Secret Recordings Be Used as Evidence in Chinese Courts?		93
		6.7.1	Are Secret Recordings Admissible in Chinese Courts?	93
		6.7.2	What Kind of Recordings Are Unlikely to Be Admitted	94
		6.7.3	What Is an Ideal Recording Evidence Like	94
	6.8	How to Collect Evidence from Internet and Social Media		95
		6.8.1	Basic Methods of Collecting Evidence from Internet and Social Media	95
		6.8.2	Strengthen the Weight of Evidence by Notarization	96
		6.8.3	Evidence Collection by Timestamp	97
		6.8.4	Evidence Collection by Blockchain	98
	6.9	Technical Examination Officer		100
		6.9.1	What Is Technical Examination Officer	100
		6.9.2	Who Can Be the Technical Examination Officer	101
		6.9.3	Effectiveness of the Opinion of the Technical Examination Officer	101

		6.9.4	How Does the Technical Examination Officer System Work	102
	6.10	\multicolumn{2}{l	}{Expert Opinions—Professional Opinions Provided by Neutral Judicial Expertise Institutions}	102
		6.10.1	What Is Expert Opinion	103
		6.10.2	Who Can Be the Expert	103
		6.10.3	How to Initiate the Appraisal and Examination	104
		6.10.4	How to Select the Expert	104
		6.10.5	What Is the Effect of Expert Opinion	104
		6.10.6	Costs of Appraisal and Examination	105
	6.11	\multicolumn{2}{l	}{Evidence Investigation and Collection by the Court—A Complement to the Presentation of Evidence by the Parties Themselves}	106
		6.11.1	What Evidence Can Be Investigated and Collected by the Court	106
		6.11.2	How to Apply to the Court for Evidence Investigation and Collection	107
		6.11.3	How Does the Court Investigate and Collect Evidence	107
		6.11.4	The Probative Force of the Evidence Collected by Courts	107
	6.12	\multicolumn{2}{l	}{How Do Chinese Courts Assist Foreign Courts in Investigation and Evidence Collection}	108
		6.12.1	Assistance in Investigation and Evidence Collection Under the Hague Evidence Taking Convention	108
		6.12.2	Assistance in Investigation and Evidence Collection Under Bilateral Treaties	110
	6.13	\multicolumn{2}{l	}{Evidence Preservation—The Court's Preservation of Evidence that May Be Destroyed}	110
		6.13.1	What Is Evidence Preservation	110
		6.13.2	Comparison Between Evidence Preservation and Evidence Investigation and Collection by Courts	111
		6.13.3	Application and Examination of Evidence Preservation	111
		6.13.4	The Method and Effect of Evidence Preservation	112
	6.14	\multicolumn{2}{l	}{Evidence Discovery and Disclosure in China?—Evidence Presentation Order}	113
		6.14.1	What Is Evidence Presentation Order	113
		6.14.2	Is China's Evidence Presentation Order Equal to the Evidence Discovery and Disclosure?	114
		6.14.3	How to Apply to the Court for an Evidence Presentation Order	114
		6.14.4	Application in Practice	115

		6.14.5	Prospect and Suggestions	115
	6.15		How to Keep Evidence Confidential in Litigation	116
		6.15.1	Try to Avoid Submitting Evidence Containing Confidential Information	116
		6.15.2	Cover Up the Confidential Part	116
		6.15.3	Request the Judge to Narrow Down the Scope of Evidence Presentation	117
		6.15.4	Request a Non-public Court Trial or Evidence Examination	117
		6.15.5	What if the Court Orders the Parties to Present Unsubmitted Evidence?	118
7	**Class Action in China?—Representative Litigation**			121
	7.1		What Is Representative Litigation	121
	7.2		Who Will Be Bound by the Court Judgment in the Representative Litigation	122
	7.3		How to Determine the Representative	122
	7.4		China's Representative Litigation in Practice	123
	7.5		Representative Litigation for Securities Disputes	123
		7.5.1	The Newly Revised Securities Law Introduces the Representative Litigation System for Securities Dispute Resolution	124
		7.5.2	Basic Procedures for Starting the Representative Litigation for Securities Disputes	125
		7.5.3	Special Requirements for Starting Representative Litigation for Securities Disputes	125
		7.5.4	How to Determine the Scope of the Plaintiff	126
		7.5.5	How to Determine the Representative in Securities Disputes	126
		7.5.6	What Special Rights Does the Representative Enjoy in Securities Disputes	128
		7.5.7	Practice and Future Prospects	128
8	**Civil Public Interest Litigation**			131
	8.1		What Is Civil Public Interest Litigation	131
	8.2		Public Interest Litigation Versus Private Interest Litigation	132
	8.3		Who May File a Civil Public Interest Litigation	133
		8.3.1	Social Organizations	133
		8.3.2	Procuratorates	134
	8.4		Announcement Is Required for a Public Interest Litigation	135
	8.5		The Competent Administrative Department Shall Be Informed of the Public Interest Litigation	135
	8.6		The Court May Intervene in the Legal Proceedings with a More Proactive Manner	135

9	**Property Preservation and Act Preservation**			139
	9.1	Property Preservation—The Key to Prevent Defendants from Transferring/Hiding Property		139
		9.1.1	What Is Property Preservation	139
		9.1.2	How to Apply for the Property Preservation?	140
		9.1.3	How Chinese Courts Implement the Property Preservation	141
		9.1.4	The Validity Period of Property Preservation	142
		9.1.5	The Consequences of Violating a Court Order	142
		9.1.6	Application Fee Charged by the Court	143
		9.1.7	Providing Guarantee and Relevant Fees	143
		9.1.8	Our Advice	143
	9.2	Act Preservation—China's "Interlocutory Injunction"		144
		9.2.1	What Is Act Preservation	144
		9.2.2	How Chinese Courts Examine the Application for Act Preservation	145
		9.2.3	The Validity Period of Act Preservation	146
		9.2.4	The Consequences of Violating a Court Order	146
		9.2.5	The Consequences of an Erroneous Application for Act Preservation	147
10	**Enforcement**			149
	10.1	What Is Enforcement and Some Basic Points		150
	10.2	China Has Long Been Plagued by the "Difficulty in Enforcement"		151
	10.3	Track Down and/or Freeze the Property of the Party Subject to Enforcement Through the Information Network System		152
	10.4	Dispose of the Property of the Party Subject to Enforcement Through Online Auction		153
	10.5	Restrictions and Punishments on the Party Subject to Enforcement		155
	10.6	Recognition and Enforcement of Foreign Arbitral Awards—A Bright Future Ahead		157
		10.6.1	Proactive Practice of the New York Convention	157
		10.6.2	Other Supporting Systems	157
		10.6.3	Time Limit and Application Fee	158
		10.6.4	Practice	158
	10.7	Recognition and Enforcement of Foreign Court Judgments—A Pathway Worth a Try		159
		10.7.1	Bilateral Treaties or Reciprocal Relationship—Preconditions for the Recognition and Enforcement of Foreign Court Judgments	159
		10.7.2	Significant Relaxation of the Criteria for Determining a Reciprocal Relationship	159

	10.7.3	Other Rules Stipulated by the Conference Summary 2022	160
	10.7.4	Practice and Future Prospects	161

11 Settlement and Mediation ... 163
11.1 The Difference Between Settlement and Mediation ... 163
11.2 Mediation Organized by Organizations Other Than the Court ... 164
11.3 Self-admission in Settlement and Mediation ... 165
11.4 Confidentiality in Settlement and Mediation ... 165

About the Author

Chenyang Zhang is a partner of Tian Yuan Law Firm. Chenyang Zhang specializes in dispute resolution, including litigation, arbitration and alternative dispute resolution. In addition, Mr. Zhang is experienced in commercial background investigation and evidence collection. Prior to joining Tian Yuan Law Firm, Chenyang Zhang has worked with Yuanhe Partners and King and Wood Mallesons.

Chenyang Zhang has extensive experience in commercial litigation, bankruptcy/insolvency matters and intellectual property. Chenyang Zhang's clients include large-scale Chinese enterprises such as Sinopec, CNOOC, Industrial and Commercial Bank of China, Capital Airport Group, Cinda Investment, as well as trading and investment enterprises from the USA, Germany, Australia, India, Turkey, Brazil, UAE, Thailand, Malaysia, Singapore and other countries or regions. Chenyang Zhang has represented his clients in over one hundred cases before the Supreme People's Court of China, other local courts, as well as arbitral institutions such as China International Economic and Trade Arbitration Commission.

Cases and experiences of Chenyang Zhang can be found in the case list below.

Chenyang Zhang obtained his LL.B. in 2011 and LL.M. in 2013 from China Foreign Affairs University respectively. Chenyang Zhang's working languages include Chinese (Mandarin, native) and English (fluent).

A Selection of Chenyang Zhang's Cases and Experiences

- Representing an Australian mining company in the arbitration proceeding for a dispute on coal source exploration and investment agreement against a large state-owned coal mining company of China. More than 500 million RMB was involved in this case.
- Representing enterprises from the USA, Germany, Singapore, UAE, Qatar, South Africa and etc. to collect debts against enterprises in mainland China.
- Participating in a series of disputes on real estates between a real estate company and its Japanese shareholder. More than 300 million RMB was involved in this case.
- Participating in a series of arbitration proceedings for disputes on the agreements about investing in Africa as executed by a subsidiary investment company of a state-owned company. More than 300 million RMB was involved in this case.
- Representing a world-renowned manufacturer of elevator in a dispute on elevator purchase contract against a large retail enterprise. Around 20 million RMB was involved in this case.
- Participating in the arbitration proceeding for a dispute on agriculture products sale and purchasing agreement between a Thai agriculture company and a trade company in Jiangsu Province. More than 20 million RMB was involved in this case.
- Representing a well-known US retailer in a series of arbitration proceedings for disputes on sale and purchasing agreements.
- Participating in a series of patent infringement disputes between a multinational household appliance company and an equipment manufacturing company in Zhejiang Province. More than 30 million RMB was involved in this case.
- Representinging a number of entities affiliated to Chinese Academy of Sciences to dissolve poor-performing enterprises they invested in.

- Serving as a PRC law expert witness in an international trade-related arbitration case heard by Hong Kong International Arbitration Center.

Publications

The Nationality of the Arbitral Award of International Commercial Arbitration, graduation thesis for master of laws

Implication on Judging the Validity of Guarantee Contract from the Regulation of Foreign Exchange Administration for Cross-Border Guarantee, see Minsheng Weekly of People's Daily

Rules on Private Sector Borrowing Shall Apply to Entrustment Loans, see Minsheng Weekly of People's Daily

A series of introductions on the judicial system of China, see: https://www.chinajusticeobserver.com/contributors/chenyang_zhang

Lectures and Seminars

Enforcing foreign judgments in China, lecture on following webinars:

"Germany-China Debt Collection: Enforcing Foreign Judgments and Arbitral Awards" held by China Justice Observer on May 27, 2022

"Portugal-China Debt Collection: Enforcing Foreign Judgments" held by China Justice Observer on October 11, 2022

How to Collect Your Debt in China, lecture on following webinars:

"Turkey-China Debt Collection" held by China Justice Observer on 20 October 2022

"Italy-China Debt Collection" held by China Justice Observer on 24 October 2022

"Nigeria-China Debt Collection" held by China Justice Observer on November 21, 2022

e-mail: zhangchenyang@tylaw.com.cn; zhangchenyang.legal@aliyun.com

Abbreviations

SPC	The Supreme People's Court of the People's Republic of China 中华人民共和国最高人民法院
CPL	Civil Procedure Law of the People's Republic of China (Latest revision: 2021) 《中华人民共和国民事诉讼法》(2021年最后一次修订)
CPL Revision Draft 2022	Draft of Revision of the Civil Procedure Law of the People's Republic of China (published in December 2022) 《中华人民共和国民事诉讼法(修正草案)》(2022年12月发布)
Judicial Interpretation of CPL	Interpretation of the Supreme People's Court on the Application of the Civil Procedure Law of the People's Republic of China (Latest revision: 2022) 《最高人民法院关于适用<中华人民共和国民事诉讼法>的解释》(2022 年最后一次修订)
Judicial Interpretation on Civil Evidence	Provisions of the Supreme People's Court on Evidence for Civil Procedure (Latest revision: 2019, Fa Shi [2019] No. 19) 《最高人民法院关于民事诉讼证据的若干规定》(2019 年最后一次修订, 法释 (2019) 19号)

Judicial Interpretation on Property Preservation	Provisions of the Supreme People's Court on Several Issues Relating to Handling of Property Preservation Cases by People's Courts (Revised in 2020, Fa Shi [2016] No. 22) 《最高人民法院关于人民法院办理财产保全案件若干问题的规定》(2020 年修订, 法释 (2016) 22 号)
Conference Summary 2022	Conference Summary of the Symposium on Foreign-Related Commercial and Maritime Trials of Courts Nationwide (Promulgated in 2022) 《全国法院涉外商事海事审判工作座谈会会议纪要》(2022 年颁布)

Chapter 1
Some Basic Concepts and Systems

Abstract Before we start to explore specific aspects and procedures of civil litigation in China, it is necessary to look through some basic concepts and systems under the Chinese law first. This chapter will cover such aspects as China's 4-level court system, how many instances will a civil case go through, how cases are numbered and what information does the case number reveal, what is cause of action and its functions, how much court fee do the parties need to pay, and an overview of the whole process of civil litigation in China. At last, a brief introduction to Chinese lawyers' role and function is presented as well. We hope this chapter could help readers build a framework of China's civil litigation system and go through other sections of this book more efficiently.

1.1 China's Court System—Magnificent 4-Level Pyramid

On the basis of Chinese traditional judicial system, recent years have seen many newly established Chinese courts. Therefore, it seems difficult for those who are unfamiliar with China's court system to have a comprehensive understanding of the Chinese court system. In this regard, we depict this latest structure of China court hierarchy.

1.1.1 The 4-Level System of Chinese Courts

Chinese courts are divided into 4 levels and presidents of Chinese courts at different levels are elected by the people's congress (the organ of state power exercising legislative powers, etc.) at corresponding level as below:

- The Supreme People's Court (SPC) (whose president is elected by the National People's Congress)
- High people's court (whose president is elected by provincial people's congress)
- Intermediate people's court (whose president is generally elected by municipal people's congress)

- Primary people's court (whose president is generally elected by people's congress at county-level and district-level)

According to our incomplete statistics based on information from the official website of the SPC (https://www.court.gov.cn/), China Court Trial Online (http://tingshen.court.gov.cn/) and other information sources, nowadays there are approximately 3531 courts in Mainland China, including the SPC, about 32 high people's courts, 413 intermediate people's courts and 3085 primary people's courts.

In addition, it is often seen in news that China has newly established some "tribunals". These "tribunals" are not independent courts, but only integral parts of the courts. The judgments made by the tribunals are deemed as those made by the courts to which they belong. For example, The First Intermediate People's Court of Beijing Municipality established Beijing Bankruptcy Tribunal, the ruling of which is deemed as a ruling rendered by The First Intermediate People's Court of Beijing Municipality.

1.1.2 The Classification of Chinese Courts

Chinese courts can be divided into three categories: the SPC, local courts, and specialized courts.

1.1.2.1 The SPC

The SPC is the judicial organ at the highest level in China. In addition to hearing specific cases, the SPC is also responsible for formulating judicial interpretations. Judicial interpretations are a set of rules formulated to harmonize the courts' understanding of specific legal provisions and to unify the trial standards. In practice, they have equal effect to the law.

The SPC currently has a total of 33 permanent divisions. Most divisions are based in Beijing headquarter, while some are located in other cities, including six circuit courts and two international commercial courts.

Six circuit courts were established in Shenzhen, Shenyang, Nanjing, Zhengzhou, Chongqing, and Xi'an, which are responsible for handling cases respectively in southern, northeast, east, central, southwest and northwest part of China.[1] Cases from northern China, certain special types of cases, such as intellectual property,

---

[1] Circuits (provincial administrative regions) of six circuit courts:
The First Circuit Court: Guangdong, Guangxi, Hunan and Hainan.
The Second Circuit Court: Liaoning, Jilin and Heilongjiang.
The Third Circuit Court: Shanghai, Jiangsu, Zhejiang, Fujian and Jiangxi.
The Fourth Circuit Court: Henan, Shanxi, Hubei and Anhui.
The Fifth Circuit Court: Chongqing, Sichuan, Guizhou, Yunnan and Tibet.
The Sixth Circuit Court: Shaanxi, Gansu, Qinghai, Ningxia and Xinjiang.
Cases from Beijing, Tianjin, Hebei, Shandong and Inner Mongolia are heard by the headquarter of the SPC.

maritime disputes, and foreign-related commercial disputes are handled by the SPC headquarter. The judges of the circuit court generally rotate every two years.

Two international commercial courts were established in June 2018, respectively located in Shenzhen and Xi'an. International commercial courts mainly hear first-instance international commercial cases where the amount in controversy exceeds RMB 300 million and the parties concerned are required to agree to submit to the jurisdiction of the SPC.

It is worth noting that there are two IP-related divisions in Beijing: SPC's "Intellectual Property Division" (知识产权审判庭) (i.e. the Third Civil Division) and SPC's "Intellectual Property Court" (知识产权法庭) established in 2019. Their names are very similar in Chinese, but their functions are different. Before 2019, all kinds of intellectual property cases were handled by the Third Civil Division. After 2019, second-instance appeals with strong technical features, such as invention patents and technical secrets, are subject to jurisdiction of the newly established Intellectual Property Court; other cases and complaints or retrial cases where the appellants or petitioners are unsatisfied with the second-instance judgments rendered by the Intellectual Property Court will still be heard in the Third Civil Division.

1.1.2.2 Local Court

Local courts usually hear most of the cases in a certain area (that is, all cases except those under the jurisdiction of specialized courts). Specifically speaking, each county and district has a primary people's court, and each city, comprising several counties and/or districts will have an intermediate people's court, which is the higher court of the primary people's courts within the city. Each province, comprising several cities will have a high people's court, which is the higher court of the intermediate people's courts within the province. Above-mentioned courts are namely local courts.

China is composed of several provincial administrative regions, and the SPC is the higher court of high people's courts at provincial level.

1.1.2.3 Specialized Court

Specialized courts usually hear certain types of cases in a certain area. Since China emphasizes that all political power comes from the people and serves the people, the names of Chinese courts at different levels (including the SPC and local courts) include the word "people"(人民). However, the word, "people" is not included in the name of the specialized court. Therefore, some people joked that the specialized courts do not serve the people. Although it is just a joke, it is an effective way to distinguish between specialized courts and local courts.

The existing specialized courts in China mainly include intellectual property courts, Internet courts, financial courts and maritime courts. These courts are mainly distributed as follows:

- Intellectual Property Courts are located in: Beijing, Shanghai, Guangzhou and Haikou
- Internet Courts are located in: Beijing, Guangzhou and Hangzhou
- Financial Courts are located in: Beijing, Shanghai and Chongqing
- Maritime Courts are located in: Shanghai, Guangzhou, Tianjin, Dalian, Ningbo, Xiamen, Qingdao, Wuhan, Beihai, Haikou and Nanjing

The railway transport courts and various military courts of the People's Liberation Army of China are also specialized courts, which, however, will not be discussed here.

The level of different specialized courts varies. Among the above courts, intellectual property courts, financial courts, and maritime courts are all intermediate courts, and their corresponding higher courts are the high people's courts where the said special courts are located. However, Internet courts are primary courts, and their higher courts are the intermediate courts where they are located.

In addition, some local courts also have the characteristics of specialized courts. For example, although The Fourth Intermediate People's Court of Beijing Municipality is not a specialized court, it handles almost all foreign-related commercial cases and all arbitration judicial review cases within Beijing.

1.1.3 Separate Functions of Courts at All Levels

The first-instance civil and commercial cases are heard by courts in different levels, which is mainly determined by the type of case and the amount in controversy, and the standards in different regions are also different. Take foreign-related commercial cases in Beijing courts as an example: cases that the amount in controversy is greater than or equal to RMB 5 billion shall be heard by The High People's Court of Beijing Municipality, and other cases shall be heard by The Fourth Intermediate People's Court of Beijing Municipality.

For a long time, the SPC is mainly engaged in trial of second-instance cases and retrial cases, and barely hears first-instance cases. After the establishment of the two International Commercial Courts of the SPC in June 2018, the SPC began accepting first-instance international commercial cases. According to relevant news reports, at least 27 cases have been filed by two international commercial courts as of August 2022.

In addition, leapfrog appeal will not be sustained in a vast majority of cases in China, and the parties can only appeal to the higher court of the first instance court. The only exception is the intellectual property case with strong professionally technical feature: even if the court of first instance is an intermediate court, the appeal of second instance shall be directly heard by the SPC's "Intellectual Property Court", rather than by the high people's court at the provincial level.

(Reference provisions and information for Sect. 1.1).[2]

1.2 China's Hierarchical Trial System for Civil Cases—2 + 1 + 1

China's hierarchical trial system for civil cases can be summarized as "2 + 1 + 1", namely:

- 2: Generally, cases shall be closed after the second instance.
- 1: Under special circumstances, the parties may also apply to a higher court for retrial of the case after the final adjudication.
- 1: After the application for retrial is dismissed by the court, the parties may also apply to the procuratorate for review of the case so that the court is requested to retry the case. But the success rate is even lower.

After the application for retrial is dismissed by the court, the parties may also apply to the procuratorate for review of the case so that the court is requested to retry the case. Even after the end of the "2 + 1 + 1" procedure, the parties may still be entitled to petition in theory. But the success rate is even lower. In addition, some cases are not subject to the "2 + 1 + 1" procedure.

1.2.1 Most Cases Are Closed After the Second Instance

The meaning of "cases closed after the second instance" is that if the parties refuse to accept the first-instance judgment, they can appeal to a higher court, and the higher

---

[2] *Constitution of the People's Republic of China (Revised in 2018).*
《中华人民共和国宪法》(2018修订).
Organic Law of People's Courts of the People's Republic of China (Revised in 2018).
《中华人民共和国人民法院组织法》(2018修订).
CPL (Revised in 2021).
Provisions of the Supreme People's Court on Several Issues Concerning the Establishment of International Commercial Courts (Fa Shi [2018] No.11).
《最高人民法院关于设立国际商事法庭若干问题的规定》(法释〔2018〕11号).
Provisions of the Supreme People's Court on Several Issues Concerning Intellectual Property Court (Fa Shi [2018] No.22).
《最高人民法院关于知识产权法庭若干问题的规定》(法释〔2018〕22号).
Speech at the Third Symposium of the International Commercial Expert Committee of the SPC from Kaiyuan Tao, Vice-president of the SPC (published on 21 September 2022, see: https://cicc.court.gov.cn/html/1/218/62/164/2237.html.
最高人民法院国际商事专家委员会第三届研讨会陶凯元副院长在最高人民法院国际商事专家委员会第三届研讨会上的主题发言 *(2022年9月21日发布).*

court will conduct the second-instance trial. The second-instance judgment shall be the effective and final judgment and the parties can apply for the enforcement thereof. In addition to civil cases, criminal and administrative cases are generally also subject to the "cases closed after the second instance".

As mentioned in Sect. 1.1, Chinese courts are divided into four levels: primary, intermediate, high and supreme. Therefore, appeals against first-instance judgments rendered by primary people's courts should be tried by intermediate people's courts, and so on.

Leapfrog appeals cannot be made for most cases in China, with the only exception of intellectual property cases with strong technical attribute. Depending on the amount in controversy, the court of first instance for these cases may be either the high people's court or the intermediate people's court. Even if the court of first instance for these cases is an intermediate people's court, the second instance shall be directly tried by the Intellectual Property Court of the SPC rather than by a high people's court.

The cases allowed for leapfrog appeals are mainly civil and administrative cases related to patents, new varieties of plants, layout design of integrated circuits, technical secrets, computer software, monopoly (including administrative cases related to the granting and confirmation of patent), but first-instance civil cases related to design patents are not included herein. The main purpose of leapfrog appeal is that the SPC, as the appellate court, may unify the adjudication standards of lower courts in intellectual property cases, and avoid the improper protection of local interests by high people's courts.

As for the time limit of appeal, it is usually within 15 days from the date of service of the first-instance judgment, but for the party without domicile in China, the time limit is 30 days. According to Chinese laws, litigation-related documents formed in foreign countries need to be notarized in the country of domicile of the foreign party and authenticated by Chinese embassies/consulates in the said country. Preparing relevant documents in such a short time is also a challenge for the foreign parties.

1.2.2 Simple and Small Claim Cases Are Closed After the First Instance

For simple civil cases tried by primary people's courts, if the amount in controversy is less than 50% of the average annual salary in the previous year of the province involved, the case shall be closed after the first instance and the parties concerned shall not appeal.

It is worth noting that foreign-related civil cases shall not be forced to be closed after the first instance regardless of the amount in controversy, but rather may be subject to the second instance.

1.2.3 After the Final Trial of a Case, the Parties May also Apply for Retrial

After the final trial of a case (either the final trial after the second instance or the final trial after the first instance if no appeal is brought), that is, after the judgment has entered into force, the parties can also point out to a higher court the errors in evidence determination, application of law, litigation procedure and so on, and apply for retrial of the case. Whether a retrial procedure will commence shall be decided by a higher court after examination.

It is worth noticing that the SPC initiated a reform on the retrial system on 1 October 2021. After this day, the application for retrial against an effective judgment made by a high people's court should generally be submitted to such high people's court, rather than the SPC. Only if the effective judgment is wrong in understanding or application of law, or the effective judgment has been discussed and decided by the adjudication committee of such high people's court, the application for retrial can be submitted to the SPC. Such rules have been absorbed by the CPL Revision Draft 2022, which was published on 30 December 2022 for public comments.

In addition, to apply to the SPC for retrial, the applicant has to express the assent to the judgment's finding on basic facts, main evidence and litigation procedures. As far as we understand, such reform shows that the SPC will mainly focus on issues related to understanding and application of law. Lower-level courts should be responsible for facts finding.

The difference between applying for retrial and appeal is that, as long as the parties appeal according to law, the court will certainly conduct the second instance, while the application for retrial will be subject to the court's examination and approval before the retrial procedure can be initiated. Before the initiation of the retrial procedure, the original judgment should also be continued to be enforced. Given that judgments to be reviewed in retrial have already become effective, Chinese courts impose strict control over the retrial procedure. According to incomplete statistics and personal experience, about 10% of retrial applications can be approved by the court.

Regarding the time limit for applying for retrial, regardless of Chinese or foreign parties, they generally should apply for retrial within 6 months after the judgment takes effect.

1.2.4 After the Application for Retrial Is Dismissed, the Parties May also Apply to the Procuratorate for Case Review

If the application for retrial is dismissed by a higher court, the parties may also apply to the procuratorate at the same level with the court of last resort for case review. If the procuratorate considers that there are indeed errors in the case, it may report the case to the higher procuratorate which shall then lodge a protest against the court at its corresponding level, so that the court may retry the case. The procuratorate may also make procuratorial suggestions to the court of last resort, and the court of last resort may decide whether to retry the case at its sole discretion.

Applying to the procuratorate for case review is the last resort of the parties. As the procuratorate respects the certainty of the court's judgment, it is often more difficult to apply to the procuratorate for case review than to apply to a higher court for retrial.

Regarding the time limit for applying to the procuratorate for case review, regardless of Chinese or foreign parties, they should generally apply for case review within two years after the application for retrial is dismissed by the court.

1.2.5 After the End of the "2 + 1 + 1" Procedure, the Parties May Still Be Entitled to Petition in Theory

After the end of the "2 + 1 + 1" procedure, the parties have exhausted their litigation rights and it is difficult to initiate any legal proceedings. However, according to the CPL, courts can take the initiative to review errors in their own judgments and lower courts' judgments, and retry cases involved. Therefore, in theory, the parties can keep petitioning to attract the attention of the court. However, the success rate of such petition is extremely low.

In practice, courts usually set up mailboxes to receive letters from representatives of national and local people's congresses. Therefore, the parties can invite the representatives to assist in petitioning, but this only contributes to the success rate in a limited extent.

1.2.6 Cases that Are not Subject to the "2 + 1 + 1" Procedure

Although the aforementioned simple and small claim cases shall be closed after the first instance, application for retrial and review by the procuratorate may still be initiated for such cases. However, cases of setting aside the arbitral award and cases of confirming the validity of the arbitration agreement shall not only be closed after the first instance, application for retrial and review by the procuratorate are also prohibited, and even the court is not allowed to correct errors and conduct retrial by itself. It can be understood as Chinese courts respect arbitration and try to avoid the uncertainty of the judicial review on arbitration.

In addition, the "2 + 1 + 1" procedure is not applicable to special procedure cases such as the determination of citizens with no capacity for civil conduct.

(Reference provisions and information for Sect. 1.2).[3]

---

[3] *CPL (Revised in 2021): Article 10, 165, 166, 171, 205, 206, 207, 212, 216, 276.*
CPL Revision Draft 2022: Article 210.
Judicial Interpretation of CPL (Revised in 2022).

1.3 Case Numbering System of Chinese Courts—"Secret Signal" in Case Number

The case number in Chinese courts consists of a set of elements showing the year of case acceptance, the court, the case type code and the serial number. You can easily find such information with knowledge of case numbering method.

1.3.1 Basic Format of Case Number

The general format of the case number in Chinese courts is as follows: (year of case acceptance) + court code + case type code + serial number. Take "(2017) Jing 04 Min Zhong No. 367" ((2017)京04民终367号) as an example:

- "(2017)" is the year of case acceptance
- "Jing 04" is the court code, referring to The Fourth Intermediate People's Court of Beijing Municipality
- "Min Zhong" is the case type code, referring to the civil case of second instance
- "No. 367" is the serial number

Therefore, "(2017) Jing 04 Min Zhong No. 367" refers to the 367th civil case of second instance accepted by The Fourth Intermediate People's Court of Beijing Municipality in 2017.

Next, we will walk you through the compilation of the court code and the case type code respectively.

1.3.2 Compilation Rules for Court Codes

Before 2016, there was no uniform court code rule in China, and a court generally chose one or two Chinese characters from the full name of the court as the court code

---

Notice of the Supreme People's Court on Promulgation of the Implementing Measures for Improving the Pilot Reform of Functional Positioning of Trial Level of Courts at Four Levels (Fa [2021] No.242): Article 11, 12.
《最高人民法院关于印发＜关于完善四级法院审级职能定位改革试点的实施办法＞的通知》(法〔2021〕242号).
Provisions of the Supreme People's Court on Several Issues Concerning Intellectual Property Court (Fa Shi [2018] No.22).
《最高人民法院关于知识产权法庭若干问题的规定》(法释〔2018〕22号).
Rules on Supervision over Civil Proceedings by People's Procuratorates: Article 20.
《人民检察院民事诉讼监督规则》
Provisions of the Supreme People's Court on Several Issues relating to the Hearing of Cases Involving Judicial Review of Arbitration (Fa Shi [2017] No.22): Article 20.
《最高人民法院关于审理仲裁司法审查案件若干问题的规定》(法释〔2017〕22号).

in the case number. This practice not only made the court code chaotic and difficult for identification, but also produced many duplicate codes. For example, The High People's Court of Beijing Municipality is a provincial high court, and The Primary People's Court of Gaomi County of Shandong Province is a county-level grass-root court, but codes of both courts are "Gao (高 in Chinese, literally means "high" in English)". Seeing the word "Gao" in the case number, people cannot determine which court the case comes from, or are even more likely to think that the case comes from the SPC, since in Chinese pinyin, the SPC pronounces "Zui Gao Ren Min Fa Yuan", which also includes the word "Gao".

Since 2016, China has begun to implement uniform court code compilation rules. Through this set of rules, each court has a unique code, from which we can be directly informed of the court's location, hierarchy, category and other information. The basic framework of this set of rules is:

The abbreviation of the province where the court is located (1 Chinese character) + administrative division code/special code (2 or 4 Arabic numerals).

Each provincial administrative region in China has a fixed abbreviation of one Chinese character (for example, Beijing is abbreviated as "Jing" (京) and Guangdong is abbreviated as "Yue" (粤)). The code of all high courts is the abbreviation of the Chinese character of the province in which they are located (but the abbreviation for courts in Inner Mongolia (in Chinese pinyin, Neimenggu) is "Nei" (内) instead of "Meng"). There are 6-digit codes for courts in all administrative divisions above the county level in China. Among them, the 1st and 2nd digits refer to the province, the 3rd and 4th digits refer to the city, while the 5th and 6th digits refer to the district/county. The code for the intermediate court needs to be affixed with the 3rd and 4th digits after the provincial abbreviation, while the code for the primary court needs to be affixed with the 3rd to 6th digits. The code of the Supreme People's Court is "Zui Gao Fa". The following table intuitively illustrates the compilation of court codes at all levels:

Court level	Court name	Abbr. of the provincial administrative region	Administrative division code	Court code
Supreme	The Supreme People's Court (最高人民法院)	/	/	**Zui Gao Fa** (最高法)
High	The High People's Court of Guangdong Province (广东省高级人民法院)	**Yue** (粤)	440000	**Yue** (粤)
Intermediate	The Intermediate People's Court of Shenzhen City of Guangdong Province (广东省深圳市中级人民法院)	**Yue** (粤)	440300	**Yue 03** (粤03)

(continued)

1.3 Case Numbering System of Chinese Courts—"Secret Signal" in Case … 11

(continued)

Court level	Court name	Abbr. of the provincial administrative region	Administrative division code	Court code
Primary	The Primary People's Court of Futian District of Shenzhen City, Guangdong Province (广东省深圳市福田区人民法院)	Yue (粤)	440304	**Yue 0304** (**粤0304**)

The code of the specialized court should also begin with the abbreviated Chinese character of the province where it is located, and the subsequent Arabic numerals are generally used to indicate the category of the court. Similarly, we use a table for illustration:

Court level	Court name	Administrative region and its abbr.	Court category	Court category code	Court code
Intermediate	The Railway Transportation Intermediate Court of Guangzhou (广州铁路运输中级法院)	Guangdong Province (**Yue**) (广东省(粤))	Railway transport	71	**Yue 71** (**粤71**)
Intermediate	Qingdao Maritime Court (青岛海事法院)	Shandong Province (**Lu**) (山东省(鲁))	Maritime	72	**Lu 72** (**鲁72**)
Intermediate	Beijing Intellectual Property Court (北京知识产权法院)	Beijing Municipality (**Jing**) (北京市(京))	Intellectual property	73	**Jing 73** (**京73**)
Intermediate	Shanghai Financial Court (上海金融法院)	Shanghai Municipality (**Hu**) (上海市(沪))	Finance	74	**Hu 74** (**沪74**)

The SPC has published the code list of all courts in Mainland China on its official website and updated it several times (for more details, see http://www.court.gov.cn/fabu-xiangqing-14970.html). The last update was on 29 June 2016.

1.3.3 Compilation Rules for Case Type Codes

Case type codes, like court codes, did not have uniform rules until 2016. Since then, the rules have been revised several times. According to the existing rules, all cases of

Chinese courts are divided into 11 categories, such as criminal cases, civil cases and administrative cases. Each category of cases can be further subdivided into several sub-categories. Each sub-category has a case type code, which is composed entirely of Chinese characters. Take civil cases (Category 3) as an example:

Case type	Case type code
3. Civil cases	/
3.1 Civil cases of first instance (民事一审案件)	Min Chu (民初)
3.2 Civil cases of second instance (民事二审案件)	Min Zhong (民终)
3.3 Civil cases of adjudication supervision (民事审判监督案件)	/
3.3.1 Civil cases of retrial by ex officio (民事依职权再审审查案件)	Min Jian (民监)
3.3.2 Civil cases of retrial by application (民事申请再审审查案件)	Min Shen (民申)
3.3.3 Civil cases of retrial by (the procuratorate's) protest (民事抗诉再审审查案件)	Min Kang (民抗)
3.3.4 Civil retrial cases (民事再审案件)	Min Zai (民再)
……	
3.5 Cases of special procedures	/
…… 3.5.2 Cases of declaration of disappearance or death (宣告失踪、死亡案件)	Min Te (民特)
…… 3.5.12 Cases of setting aside arbitral award (撤销仲裁裁决案件) 3.5.13 Cases of application for confirmation of the validity of arbitration agreement (申请确认仲裁协议效力案件)	
……	

From the above table, we can see that some of the case type codes are compiled according to the stage in which the case is, and some are compiled according to the way the case is initiated or the content of the case. Multiple sub-categories may share one case type code.

Most commercial cases do not have separate case type codes, but use civil case type codes. However, for the first instance commercial cases accepted by the International Commercial Court of the SPC, the special code "Shang Chu" (商初) is used. For example: "(2019) Zui Gao Fa Shang Chu No. 1" ((2019)最高法民商初1号) refers to the 1st first-instance commercial case accepted by the International Commercial Court of the SPC in 2019.

There is no separate case type code for intellectual property cases. However, in cases of invention patents and technical secrets with strong technical attribute filed after 1 January 2019, it is necessary to add a word "Zhi" (知, the first character of "intellectual property" in Chinese) before the case type code. For example: "(2019) Zui Gao Fa Zhi Min Zhong No. 2" ((2019)最高法知民终2号) refers to the 2nd second-instance civil case with strong technical attribute accepted by the SPC in 2019.

Like the court code, the case type code table can be accessed on the official website of the SPC (for more details, see http://www.court.gov.cn/zixun-xiangqing-14970.html). It was last updated on 15 July 2016.

(Reference provisions and information for Sect. 1.3).[4]

1.4 Cause of Action—Index List of Chinese Case Classification

The majority of case titles in Mainland China consist of two parts, namely the types of disputes and the information of the parties concerned, the former one of which is referred to as cause of action ("案由" in Chinese). For example, in the case of infringement upon computer software copyright, *Microsoft Corporation v. Shenzhen Lanfei Technology Co., Ltd.*, the "infringement upon computer software copyright" in the initial part is the cause of action in this case. As the index list of Chinese case classification, cause of action is a very important tool for Chinese courts.

There are multiple functions for the cause of action. First of all, there is a certain correlation between the cause of action and the competent court's jurisdiction. Secondly, the cause of action directly reflects the legal basis of the plaintiff's claim. Thirdly, for the courts, the main function of the cause of action is to divide works among different trial divisions within the courts. Fourthly, the cause of action helpfully directs courts to pay attention to hot social issues and protecting new types of rights.

1.4.1 The Development of Cause of Action in Civil Cases

Before 2001, there was no unified categorization of causes of actions in civil cases in China, and the titles of cases were summarized at the courts' own discretion in accordance with the legal relationship involved in cases. With increasing caseload and

---

[4] *Notice of the Supreme People's Court on Printing and Distributing Several Provisions on Case Number Management of People's Courts and Supporting Standards (Fa [2015] No.137).*
《最高人民法院关于印发＜关于人民法院案件案号的若干规定＞及配套标准的通知》(法〔2015〕137号).
Notice of the Supreme People's Court on Printing and Distributing the Decision on Amending Several Provisions on Case Number Management of People's Courts (Fa [2018] No.335).
《最高人民法院印发《关于修改＜关于人民法院案件案号的若干规定＞的决定》的通知》(法〔2018〕335号).

increasing complexity of the cases, in 2001, Chinese courts began to try out a uniform list of cause of action. All civil cases throughout the country must be determined within the scope of the list. However, the SPC has not explicitly explained the specific functions of the cause of action.

In 2008, the SPC updated the list of causes of action in a wide range, and explained clearly the definition and functions of the causes of action, mainly including:

(1) To reflect the legal relationship involved in the case;
(2) To facilitate the parties to understand the types of cases accepted by the courts;
(3) To standardize the distinctive function of different trial divisions within the court;
(4) To assist judges in finding evidence for trial; and
(5) To provide the legal basis for the judicial statistics.

In 2011 and 2020, the SPC extensively renewed the list of causes of action for twice. The renewal in 2020 was to coordinate with the Civil Code, which took effect on 1 January 2021.

1.4.2 How to Determine the Cause of Action in the Case

The cause of action in most cases are determined by the plaintiff when a case is filed. During the case filing, if considering that the cause of action chosen by the plaintiff is not in conformity to the nature of the dispute, the judge in the Case-filing Division can guide the plaintiff to revise the cause of action. During the trial, if the judge believes that the cause of action determined is inaccurate, the judge may change the cause of the case at his or her own discretion.

Causes of action in the list are divided into four levels, among which the causes of action at Level One covers the broadest and most general scope of cases, and the causes of action at Level Four covers the narrowest and most specific scope of cases. To illustrate more explicitly, we take relevant causes of action involved in disputes over lease contracts as examples:

Level	Cause of Action
1	Disputes over contracts, negotiorum gestorum, or unjust enrichment
2	Disputes over contracts
3	Disputes over lease contracts
4	Disputes over land lease contracts
4	Disputes over housing lease contracts
4	Disputes over vehicle lease contracts
4	Disputes over construction equipment lease contracts

According to the provisions stipulated by the SPC, the cause of action at level 4 should be given priority to apply; where there is no appropriate cause of action at level 4, the corresponding cause of action at level 3 shall be applied and so on. In practice, the most frequently used cause of action is the cause of action at level 3.

If a case involves multiple disputes, in theory, the case should have multiple causes of action. However, practically, most cases are generally titled with only one cause of action.

1.4.3 Functions of the Cause of Action

First of all, there is a certain correlation between the cause of action and the competent court's jurisdiction. In the CPL and the Interpretation of CPL, the competent courts which have jurisdiction to hear specific cases are basically determined by the cause of action. The competent trial courts may be varied depending on different causes of action. For example, in accordance with Article 28 of the Interpretation of CPL, "cases about disputes over construction contracts of construction projects" shall be tried by the courts in the place where the real estate is located. As a result, for the disputes over the decoration contract of the family housing, if the cause of action is determined to be "the dispute over construction contract of the construction project", it can be heard under the jurisdiction of the court in the place where the real property is located; however, if the cause of action is determined to be "the dispute over decoration contract", the court in the place where the real property is located may refuse to accept the case on this ground and request the parties to bring a suit to courts in the place where the defendant resides or otherwise.

Secondly, the cause of action directly reflects the legal basis of the plaintiff's claim. The plaintiff's choice of different legal basis for litigation may have a substantial impact on the outcome of the case. For example, a cargo owner asked a warehouse to store batches of goods, and the two parties entered into a warehousing storage contract. After the goods were delivered to the warehouse, the warehouse was on fire and the goods were totally damaged and lost. At this time, the cargo owner can choose either "dispute over warehouse contract" or "torts dispute" as the cause of action for litigation. However, there are significant differences between the two causes of action: (1) choosing "the dispute over warehouse contract" means that the cargo owner takes the warehouse as the defendant and requires it to assume the responsibility for breach of contract. At this time, the cargo owner only needs to prove the fact that the warehouse was on fire and the goods were lost, but unnecessary to prove the reasons causing the fire. The scope of compensation is also limited by the contract and the provisions related to contract law. (2) choosing "torts disputes" means that the cargo owner needs to take the person who caused the fire as the defendant and requires him to assume tort liability. In addition to proving the fact that the warehouse was on fire and the goods were lost, the cargo owner has to find the specific responsible person and prove the cause of the warehouse fire. Plaintiff's burden of proof in torts cases is obviously heavier. But at the same time, the cargo owner may get more compensation than the liquidated damages stipulated in the contract.

If the cause of action is determined incorrectly, but the legal basis of the plaintiff's claim is clear, the judge will not frustrate the plaintiff's claim just due to incorrect cause of action. For example, the plaintiff sues the defendant for a financing lease contract. The correct cause of action should be "the dispute over financial lease contract "; but if the plaintiff mistakenly chooses "dispute over lease contract" as the cause of action. Even if the cause of action has not been corrected, the judge should still try the case according to the relevant provisions governing the financial lease contract disputes, and would not render a judgment in favor of the defendant due to wrong cause of action.

Thirdly, for the courts, the main function of the cause of action is to divide works among different trial divisions within the courts. Taking the SPC as an example, "disputes over construction contracts for construction projects" shall be heard by the First Civil Division; and "disputes over equity transfer" shall be heard by the Second Civil Division. Because the judges in different trial divisions may have different logic or ways of thinking for the case trial, the parties can roughly learn about the specific division hearing the case according to the cause of action, and accordingly adjust their litigation strategy. For example, judges hearing commercial cases tend to be more compliant to "Rechtsschein Theorie" and tend to focus more on the context of the contract when interpreting the contract, while judges in ordinary civil division pay more attention to the balance of interests of the parties and may interpret the contract beyond the context of the contract. In addition, some courts will compile standardized trial guidelines for different kinds of cases based on the categorized cause of action, which also makes it easy for judges to form a routine format in trying certain cases.

Fourthly, the cause of action helpfully directs the courts to pay attention to hot social issues and protecting new types of rights. In recent years, there has been an increasing number of cases where women suffer from employment discrimination and sexual harassment, and these cases gain more and more public attention. Under the continuous appeal of the All-China Women's Federation, the SPC announced two more types of causes of action on 12 December 2018, namely "the dispute over equal employment rights" and "dispute over liabilities caused by sexual harassment". For the female plaintiffs in these cases, if they satisfy certain conditions, the government will consider providing them with some legal aids.

(Reference provisions and information for Sect. 1.4).[5]

---

[5] *Provisions on Causes of Action for Civil Cases (Promulgated in 2008, Revised in 2011, 2018 and 2020).*
 《民事案件案由规定》*(2008年颁布, 2011、2018、2020年修订).*

1.5 How Do Chinese Courts Charge—Court Costs

Chinese courts generally charge the case acceptance fee according to the claim amount. The case acceptance fee is charged on a progressive rate. The higher the claim amount, the lower the rate. The case acceptance fee and the application fee are generally prepaid by the plaintiff and ultimately borne by the losing party. The fees charged by Chinese courts are denominated in RMB.

1.5.1 Fee Rates of Chinese Courts

For most cases, Chinese courts charge the case acceptance fee according to the claim amount as per a progressive rate listed in the following table:

Claim amount (X)	Case acceptance fee
< RMB 10,000	RMB 50
RMB 10,000–RMB 100,000	2.5% X − RMB 200
RMB 100,000–RMB 200,000	2% X + RMB 300
RMB 200,000–RMB 500,000	1.5% X + RMB 1300
RMB 500,000–RMB 1,000,000	1% X + RMB 3800
RMB 1 million–RMB 2 million	0.9% X + RMB 4800
RMB 2 million–RMB 5 million	0.8% X + RMB 6800
RMB 5 million–RMB 10 million	0.7% X + RMB 11,800
RMB 10 million–RMB 20 million	0.6% X + RMB 21,800
> RMB 20 million	0.5% X + RMB 41,800

According to the above table, we have calculated the case acceptance fees for different claim amounts:

Claim Amount	Case Acceptance Fee
RMB 10,000	RMB 50
RMB 100,000	RMB 2300
RMB 1 million	RMB 13,800
RMB 5 million	RMB 46,800
RMB 10 million	RMB 81,800
RMB 20 million	RMB 141,800
RMB 50 million	RMB 291,800
RMB 100 million	RMB 541,800

The above rate table is not applicable to some special cases, such as:

(1) Divorce cases are charged at RMB 50–300 per case, and the specific fee is subject to the rates of local courts. If the property to be divided at the time of divorce exceeds RMB 200,000, an additional 0.5% of the part exceeding RMB 200,000 will be charged as well;
(2) Labor dispute cases are charged at RMB 10 per case. This is to reduce the cost for workers to defend their rights;
(3) Application for setting aside an arbitral award or determining the validity of an arbitration agreement will be charged at RMB 400 per case; and
(4) Application for recognition and enforcement of a foreign court judgment or arbitral award is generally charged at RMB 500 per case. In practice, some courts will charge according to the fee rates of ordinary enforcement cases (subject to a progressive rate), but these fees are not to be paid by the applicant, but are directly deducted from the respondent's property.

After the first-instance judgment is made, the party who files an appeal shall pay the case acceptance fee of the second instance according to the fee rate of the first instance. After the second-instance judgment is made, even if a party continues to apply for a retrial, generally, no additional fees will be charged any more.

In addition, if it is necessary to apply for property preservation, etc., the party concerned must pay an additional application fee. The application fee, up to RMB 5000, is also subject to a progressive rate.

1.5.2 *Special Circumstances of Fee Reduction/Exemption*

For persons with disability without stable income and other marginalized groups, Chinese courts may accept their cases free of charge. For the following three circumstances, Chinese courts will charge half of the standard rate:

(1) Where the summary procedure is applied. In practice, the number of foreign-related cases subject to summary procedure is relatively small, so foreign parties generally need to pay fees at the standard rate;
(2) Where the plaintiff withdraws the case, or the mediation between the parties succeeds. This is to encourage the parties to resolve disputes through consultation and negotiation, which reflects the importance that Chinese courts attach to mediation; and
(3) Where the defendant files a counterclaim, the court generally charges a counterclaim acceptance fee at half of the standard rate.

1.5.3 Payment Time and Method

The case acceptance fee shall be prepaid by the plaintiff/appellant, and the time limit for payment is within 7 days after receiving the notice of payment from the court. The notice of payment can be issued just after the court files the case or later. In practice, some judges even issue the notice of payment after the hearing.

The party may pay in cash or by bank transfer at the court or at the designated bank, or remit money to the designated account of the court. In the past two years, Chinese courts have begun to accept mobile payment by QR code scanning, which provides a lot of convenience to the parties.

If the party fails to pay the case acceptance fee in full on schedule, it shall be deemed that the party has withdrawn the case/appeal.

1.5.4 The Court Costs Shall Be Borne by the Losing Party

The losing party shall ultimately bear the court costs, unless the winning party voluntarily agrees to bear part of the costs. If only some of the claims for relief are supported by the court, the court generally orders both parties to bear the court costs jointly based on the proportion of the amount supported by the court to the total claim amount.

After the judgment takes effect, the court shall refund the court costs prepaid by the winning party, and then recover the same from the losing party. However, in practice, some courts fail to strictly implement this provision for various reasons, but combine the court costs with the amount supported by the court, and require the winning party to get compensated from the subsequent enforcement procedure. This undoubtedly increases the financial burden and risk of the winning party. Therefore, the winning party needs to maintain closer contact with the court and repeatedly urge the court to handle the refund according to law.

For cases where the plaintiff applies for withdrawal of the lawsuit, the case acceptance fee shall be borne by the plaintiff itself. For cases where both parties have reached a settlement, the assumption of court costs shall be determined by both parties through negotiation, and if the negotiation fails, the assumption of court costs shall be decided by the court.

(Reference provisions and information for Sect. 1.5).[6]

---

[6] *Judicial Interpretation of CPL (Revised in 2022): Article 207.*
Measures for the Payment of Litigation Fees.
《诉讼费用交纳办法》

1.6 General Process of Civil Litigation in China

In China, the process of a civil case under ordinary procedure generally includes the following steps:

(1) The plaintiff brings a lawsuit with the competent court, and the court accepts the case and determines the judges for case trial;
(2) The court serves court documents on the parties and wait for the defense of the defendant;
(3) The court resolves the dispute over jurisdiction (if any);
(4) The court arranges the exchange of evidence and the pretrial conference (if any);
(5) The court conducts the court hearing;
(6) The court makes and renders (serves) the judgment;
(7) The party dissatisfied with the judgment appeals (if any), and the second-instance court makes and renders (serves) the final judgment according to the prescribed procedure; and
(8) The party dissatisfied with the final judgment may also apply for a retrial by the court and/or a reexamination by the procuratorate, which is very difficult though.

In addition to ordinary procedure, there is summary procedure applicable to simple civil cases with clear-cut facts, rights and obligations and easy-to-resolve dispute tried by primary courts and dispatched tribunals thereof, and the trial process of summary procedure will be simplified to a certain extent (for summary procedure, see Sect. 5.6). Furthermore, some cases are under special procedures (such as verification of voter qualification), to which special provisions in the Chinese law shall apply, but we will not discuss special procedures here for the time being.

This section briefly introduces the trial process of cases under ordinary procedure, providing readers a quick overview on the framework of China's civil procedure rules. To learn more about each part of the process, please refer to other chapters and sections.

1.7 Chinese Lawyers in Civil Litigation

Foreign parties may entrust Chinese lawyers or their own staff as agents to deal with civil litigation cases in China. Compared with the staff, Chinese lawyers are more familiar with Chinese laws, litigation procedures and judicial practice, and are entitled to some privileges in terms of investigation and collection of evidence. The Chinese law imposes stringent confidentiality obligations on lawyers. Chinese lawyers may charge their principals by various modes, and a reasonable charging mode will help motivate lawyers to reach their best potential. We believe that Chinese lawyers are highly dependable and trustworthy partners for foreign principals.

1.7 Chinese Lawyers in Civil Litigation

1.7.1 Formulating Evidence Presentation Strategies Is One of the Core Tasks of Chinese Lawyers

Chinese lawyers, like lawyers in any other jurisdiction, need to understand the facts of the case, conduct legal analysis, and then formulate litigation strategies, among which, formulating evidence presentation strategies is a quite signature task of Chinese lawyers.

As the Chinese law adopts the basic evidence rule of "the burden of proof lies upon the party asserting a proposition", the parties are not required to take the initiative to disclose any evidence against themselves (for burden of proof, see Sect. 6.2). In addition, the time limit of evidence presentation in China is also relatively flexible (for time limit of evidence presentation, see Sect. 6.3). Therefore, the parties do not have to present all the evidence at the beginning of the lawsuit, but should formulate evidence presentation strategies in advance according to the circumstances of the case and the working habits of the judges. For example:

Some "double-edged sword" evidence contains both favorable and unfavorable content. Whether and when to submit such evidence, and how to explain the unfavorable contents contained therein may have a significant impact on the outcome of the case. In some circumstances, the parties need to present all the evidence immediately to make a preemptive move. However, sometimes the parties have to deliberately hold back some evidence, so that they can act according to the other party's evidence presentation, and even lure the other party into presenting certain "double-edged sword" evidence.

The evidence presentation strategy has a great influence on the court trial and even the final judgment. Undoubtedly, the evidence presentation strategy must be formulated on a case-by-case basis according to the circumstances of the case, the other party and the judges involved. Therefore, the contribution of a Chinese lawyer who is proficient in laws, familiar with business practices and understands judicial practice to the parties is self-evident.

1.7.2 Chinese Lawyers Can Investigate and Collect Evidence on the Strength of a Court Investigation Order

When the evidence is possessed by a third party (especially a government department) and it is objectively difficult for the parties to obtain it, the parties can apply with the court for investigation and collection of evidence. In practice, some courts can grant a lawyer investigation order, and the lawyer holding the order may collect evidence from the investigated person. Compared with the investigation and collection of evidence by the court, this method greatly improves the efficiency of evidence collection and grants the parties a certain autonomy as well (for investigation and collection of evidence by the court and lawyer investigation order, see Sect. 6.11).

However, most courts only grant such investigation orders to Chinese lawyers representing the party. If the agent entrusted by the party is not a Chinese lawyer, generally, he/she may not be able to obtain an investigation order granted by the court. Therefore, entrusting Chinese lawyers for representation is of great help to the parties in investigating and collecting evidence.

1.7.3 Confidentiality Obligations of Chinese Lawyers

The Law of the People's Republic of China on Lawyers (hereinafter referred to as the "Law on Lawyers") expressly stipulates that: a lawyer shall keep confidential the secrets of the state and trade secrets that he comes to know during his legal practice and shall not divulge the privacy of the parties concerned. A lawyer shall keep confidential the things and information that he comes to know during his legal practice which his client or another person does not want other people to know. In addition to the Law on Lawyers, other administrative regulations and the self-discipline provisions of bar associations also require lawyers to strictly abide by the confidentiality obligations. If a lawyer violates the confidentiality obligations, the party concerned can complain to bar associations and/or administrative regulation departments (local judicial bureaus), and even file a claim against the law firm where the lawyer works. If the circumstances are serious, the party concerned may also report the case to the public security organ and request that the lawyer be held criminally responsible.

Whether Chinese lawyers enjoy the attorney-client privilege, that is, whether Chinese lawyers will be required to disclose the communication records with the principals, is also a question worthy of discussion. Under the basic evidence rule of "the burden of proof lies upon the party asserting a proposition", there are only few circumstances where Chinese courts may force a party to present evidence (for evidence presentation order, see Sect. 6.14). Generally, the communication records between the lawyers and the principals are not the evidence that plays a decisive role in finding the facts of the case as understood by Chinese courts. Of course, Chinese courts must also consider the legal provisions on the lawyers' confidentiality obligations. Therefore, we believe that under most circumstances, Chinese lawyers do not need to disclose their communication records with the principals to the court. In practice, we have not yet encountered such a request made by the court as well.

It should be noted that Chinese lawyers are not subject to any confidentiality obligation for facts and information about crimes to be or being committed by the principals or others that endanger national security, public security and seriously endanger the personal safety of others.

1.7.4 Charging Modes of Chinese Lawyers

Chinese lawyers may charge by the hour, on a flat fee basis, by the result of the case (also known as a contingency fee), on a "flat fee + contingency fee" basis, etc. The specific charging mode is subject to the consultation between the principal and the lawyer.

Under the "flat fee + contingency fee" mode, the principal needs to pay a fixed amount of attorney's fee first. If the case results meet the conditions agreed in the contract, the principal then need to pay the contingency fee (generally calculated according to a certain proportion of the amount supported by the court); if the case results fail to meet the conditions agreed, the parties do not need to pay the contingency fee. This charging mode not only guarantee a fixed income for lawyers, but also helps motivate lawyers to reach their full potential, and makes it easier for principals to estimate the litigation cost. Therefore, the "flat fee + contingency fee" mode is the preferred charging mode for principals in Mainland China.

(Reference provisions and information for Sect. 1.7).[7]

Open Access This chapter is licensed under the terms of the Creative Commons Attribution 4.0 International License (http://creativecommons.org/licenses/by/4.0/), which permits use, sharing, adaptation, distribution and reproduction in any medium or format, as long as you give appropriate credit to the original author(s) and the source, provide a link to the Creative Commons license and indicate if changes were made.

The images or other third party material in this chapter are included in the chapter's Creative Commons license, unless indicated otherwise in a credit line to the material. If material is not included in the chapter's Creative Commons license and your intended use is not permitted by statutory regulation or exceeds the permitted use, you will need to obtain permission directly from the copyright holder.

---

[7] *The Law of the People's Republic of China on Lawyers (Latest revision: 2017): Article 38.*
《中华人民共和国律师法》(2017年最后一次修订).

Chapter 2
Jurisdiction

Abstract Determining the competent court is the first step to bring a lawsuit. For such purpose, two questions are to be answered: the court of which level has jurisdiction (i.e., the hierarchical jurisdiction) and the court of which place has jurisdiction (i.e., territorial jurisdiction). In terms of hierarchical jurisdiction, Chinese courts determine the hierarchy of the competent court mainly according to the case type and the disputed amount, and have formulate specific standards for this purpose. However, these standards may be revised from time to time, and it is necessary for the parties to verify pertinent standards before filing a case. Generally, the parties cannot change the level of the competent court by agreement, that is, to agree on the trial of a case by a court of another level different from that stipulated by the law, unless the agreement selects China International Commercial Court under the SPC. In some circumstances, a higher court will take the initiative to exercise jurisdiction over the cases that have been accepted by lower courts, or transfer the cases that have been accepted by it to lower courts. In terms of territorial jurisdiction, it should be analyzed according to the case type. In respect of most disputes over contracts and property rights, Chinese courts allow the parties to choose the competent court by agreement. If there is no relevant agreement, generally, the court of the place where the defendant is located will have jurisdiction over the case, and different types of cases will have other different jurisdictional connecting factors. Even if a court that accepts the case does not have jurisdiction, the party's response to actions and defense may confer jurisdiction upon the court that would have been otherwise incompetent, which is referred to as "prorogated jurisdiction" under Chinese law context. However, in respect of some specific types of cases, Chinese law does not allow the parties to choose the competent court by agreement, and the prorogated jurisdiction rules do not apply to such cases as well; such jurisdiction rules are referred to as "exclusive jurisdiction". In addition, Chinese courts will also designate specific courts to exercise cross-region jurisdiction over highly professional cases or cases with other special factors; such jurisdiction rules are referred to as "cross-region centralized jurisdiction". At last, in respect of the contract and property right litigation in which the defendant is a foreign party without domicile in China, even if the connecting factors under the general jurisdiction rules are not in China, the plaintiff may still have the right to bring a lawsuit with the court of China. If the defendant considers that the court accepting the case has no jurisdiction, it may raise an objection. If the court finds that the objection is tenable, the case will be transferred to the court with jurisdiction. If a court finds that it has no jurisdiction over an accepted case after self-examination, the court may transfer the case ex officio even though the defendant raises no objection. The court receiving the transferred case shall not re-transfer the case to another court.

2.1 Which Level of Court Does My Case Go to—Hierarchical Jurisdiction System

2.1.1 How to Determine the Hierarchical Jurisdiction

Chinese courts are divided into four levels: the SPC, high people's courts, intermediate people's courts and primary people's courts, totaling 3000+ courts. The CPL does not give specific standards for what kind of first-instance civil cases will be accepted by the foregoing courts respectively. In practice, the courts for first-instance civil cases are mainly determined by the case type and the disputed amount, and the standards vary from region to region. To this end, the SPC has formulated the hierarchical jurisdiction standards for courts nationwide for different types of cases, such as non-foreign-related civil and commercial cases, foreign-related civil and commercial cases and intellectual property cases.

At present, China's high courts only accept first-instance civil cases with a disputed amount of RMB 5 billion and above, and the number of such cases is very small. Therefore, the vast majority of first-instance civil cases are under the jurisdiction of primary or intermediate courts.

Regarding foreign-related civil and commercial cases (see Sect. 5.8), primary courts in more developed regions may have jurisdiction over cases with higher disputed amount. For example, the primary courts in Shanghai can hear foreign-related civil and commercial cases with a claim less than RMB 40 million; however, for the primary courts in Lhasa, Tibet, this standard has been reduced to RMB 20 million.

In practice, the SPC and local high courts will revise the hierarchical jurisdiction standards of different regions and cases from time to time according to the economic development. For example, foreign-related commercial cases with a disputed amount of less than RMB 5 billion in Beijing are uniformly under the jurisdiction of the Fourth Intermediate People's Court of Beijing, and the primary courts do not have jurisdiction over such cases. Given these revised standards are sometimes not published in a timely manner, a plaintiff's lawyer often needs to orally consult with the target court to verify its latest hierarchical jurisdiction standards, in addition to reviewing the provisions on hierarchical jurisdiction already published.

The hierarchical jurisdiction cannot be changed according to the agreement of the parties, which is totally different from the territorial jurisdiction. However, for first-instance international commercial cases with a disputed amount over RMB 300

2.1 Which Level of Court Does My Case Go to—Hierarchical Jurisdiction ... 27

million (the determination of international commercial cases is basically the same as that of foreign-related cases; for foreign-related cases, see Sect. 5.8), the parties may agree to choose the SPC as the competent first-instance court without being limited by the general hierarchical jurisdiction rules. Such cases will be tried by the two international commercial courts under the SPC (for details about the SPC and the First/Second International Commercial Courts, see Sect. 1.1).

If a court at a higher level deems it necessary, it may take the initiative to exercise jurisdiction over the cases already accepted by the lower court. China International Commercial Court of the SPC once tried some cases by this way. A higher court may also transfer the cases already accepted by it to the lower court. However, in practice, these practices are not frequently seen, and the jurisdiction over most cases is determined according to the hierarchical jurisdiction standards.

2.1.2 No Change of the Level of a Competent Court by Agreement and Its Exceptions

Under normal circumstances, the parties cannot, by agreement, transfer a case that falls under the jurisdiction of a court at one level to a court at another level. This is greatly different from the rules of territorial jurisdiction.

However, as introduced previously, for first-instance international commercial cases with a disputed amount over RMB 300 million, the parties may agree to choose the SPC as the competent court without being limited by the general hierarchical jurisdiction rules. Such cases will be tried by the two international commercial courts under the SPC.

2.1.3 Elevated Jurisdiction and Delegated Jurisdiction

Elevated jurisdiction: if a higher court deems it necessary, it may take the initiative to exercise jurisdiction over the cases already accepted by the lower court. China International Commercial Court of the SPC once tried some cases by this way.

Delegated jurisdiction: a higher court may also transfer the cases accepted by it to the lower court. Accordingly, if a lower court deems it necessary, it may apply to the higher court to try some cases that should have been accepted by it.

Due to the vague legal provisions on the specific conditions of elevated jurisdiction and delegated jurisdiction, in practice, the above practices of elevated jurisdiction and delegated jurisdiction are seldom seen, and the jurisdiction over most cases is determined according to hierarchical jurisdiction standards. However, as of 1 October 2021, the SPC began to implement a reform opinion aimed at reasonably determining the division of work of the 4-level courts, which made specific provisions on the conditions for elevated jurisdiction.

According to the said opinion, if any of the following problems exist in the first-instance case, the primary court or intermediate court accepting the case may apply to a higher court for elevated jurisdiction (that is, the primary court applies to the intermediate court for elevated jurisdiction; the intermediate court applies to the high court for elevated jurisdiction):

(1) Regarding the legal issues involved in the case, the provisions of the law and judicial interpretation are not clear or there are no pertinent provisions in the judicial interpretation, which need to be further clarified through judicial adjudication;
(2) There are significant differences in the application of law in the effective judgments of similar cases rendered by the higher court in past three years, or there are significant differences in the application of law in the effective judgments of similar cases rendered by other courts at the same level of the court accepting the case with the jurisdiction of the higher court, which have not been resolved as of the trial of the case; and
(3) Hearing by a higher court may better contribute to a fair trial.

In addition, if a primary court believes that: (1) the first-instance case involves major national interests or public interests, and it is not suitable to be tried by a primary court; or (2) if the case belongs to a new type of cases with difficult and complex circumstances within the jurisdiction of a higher court (i.e., the intermediate court), the primary court may also apply to the intermediate court for elevated jurisdiction. However, the intermediate court cannot, on these two grounds, apply to the high court for elevated jurisdiction regarding the first-instance case accepted by it.

To sum up, the main reason for elevated jurisdiction is to unify the application of law in similar cases. The actual operation effect of the above reform remains to be seen.

(Reference provisions and information for Sect. 2.1).[1]

---

[1] *CPL (Revised in 2021): Article 18–21, 38–39.*

Notice of the Supreme People's Court on Adjusting the Standards of High People's Courts and Intermediate People's Courts for Jurisdiction over First-instance Civil Cases (Fa Fa [2019] No.14).
《最高人民法院关于调整高级人民法院和中级人民法院管辖第一审民事案件标准的通知》(法发〔2019〕14号).

Notice of the Supreme People's Court on Adjusting the Standards of Intermediate People's Courts for Jurisdiction over First-instance Civil Cases (Fa Fa [2021] No.27).
《最高人民法院关于调整中级人民法院管辖第一审民事案件标准的通知》(法发〔2021〕27号).

Provisions of the Supreme People's Court on Several Issues Concerning Jurisdiction over Foreign-Related Civil and Commercial Cases (Fa Shi [2022] No.18).
《最高人民法院关于涉外民商事案件管辖若干问题的规定》(法释〔2022〕18号).

Notice of the Supreme People's Court on Adjusting the Standards of Local People's Courts at all Levels for Jurisdiction over First-instance Intellectual Property Civil Cases (Fa Fa [2010] No.5).
《最高人民法院关于调整地方各级人民法院管辖第一审知识产权民事案件标准的通知》(法发〔2010〕5号).

Provisions of the Supreme People's Court on Jurisdiction over First-instance Intellectual Property Civil and Administrative Cases (Fa Shi [2022] No.13).
《最高人民法院关于第一审知识产权民事、行政案件管辖的若干规定》(法释〔2022〕13号).

2.2 The Court of Which Place Has Jurisdiction—Territorial Jurisdiction System

2.2.1 Respect the Agreement Reached by the Parties

In respect of most disputes over contracts and property rights, Chinese courts allow the parties to choose the competent court of the place that is actually related to the dispute by written agreement. The written agreement can be either the jurisdiction clause in the transaction contract or a separate agreement. Generally, places that are actually related to the dispute include the defendant's domicile, the place where the contract is performed, the place where the contract is signed, the plaintiff's domicile, the location of the subject matter, etc.

The parties may choose more than one competent court in the agreement. The agreement may specify the specific name of the court or only mention a court in XX, provided that a specific court can be determined according to the agreement. If the parties agree on more than one competent court, the parties may bring a lawsuit with any one of such courts.

It should be noted that the parties can only make agreement on the territorial jurisdiction, while cannot change the hierarchical jurisdiction standards stipulated by the law. For example, for a contract case that should have been under the jurisdiction of an intermediate court, if the parties agree to choose a primary court as the competent court, then the parties' agreement on territorial jurisdiction is valid, but their agreement on hierarchical jurisdiction will be invalid; the case should still be under the jurisdiction of the intermediate court. On the contrary, for a contract case that should have been under the jurisdiction of a primary court, if the parties agree to choose an intermediate court as the competent court, then such agreement shall be invalid and the competent court shall be determined in accordance with the law, since the intermediate court has multiple jurisdictions, and it is unable to determine the competent primary court under its jurisdiction according to the agreement of the parties.

In addition, for disputes arising from the performance of (1) Sino-foreign equity joint venture contract, (2) Sino-foreign contractual joint venture contract, and (3) Sino-foreign cooperative exploration and development of natural resources contract in China, the parties may either choose Chinese courts for litigation or choose arbitration, but they shall not choose foreign courts for litigation.

When there is no agreement between the parties, for most cases, the competent court shall be determined in accordance with the following rules.

Notice of the Supreme People's Court on Promulgation of the Implementing Measures for Improving the Pilot Reform of Functional Positioning of Trial Level of Courts at Four Levels (Fa [2021] No.242): Article 4, 5.
《最高人民法院关于印发＜关于完善四级法院审级职能定位改革试点的实施办法＞的通知》(法〔2021〕242号).

2.2.2 The Place Where the Defendant Is Located: Connecting Factor for Most Cases

"Convenience for Defendants" is the most basic principle for jurisdiction allocation among Chinese courts, that is, the court of the place where the defendant is domiciled shall have jurisdiction over most cases. The basic rules of Chinese law on the determination of domicile are as follows:

(1) For a natural person, the domicile is the place where his/her household registration is made. If a natural person has been living in a place other than the domicile for more than one year consecutively at the time filing a suit or being sued, then the "habitual residence" instead of the domicile shall be used as a standard for determining the competent court.
(2) For an organization, the domicile is the place where its main business office is located. If the location of the main business office cannot be determined, the place of incorporation or registration shall be deemed as the domicile.

For convenience of expression, the domicile and the habitual residence are often collectively referred to as "location" in law and practice. This post also adopts this expression.

In practice, the main basis for determining the location of a natural person is the address recorded on the household register, ID card, and residence permit. The main basis for determining the location of an organization is the address recorded in the business license and registration certificate. If a party can submit sufficient evidence to prove that the location of one party is inconsistent with that recorded in the certificate or business license (such as photos of the main business office, and premises lease contract), the Chinese court can also determine the location of the party based on such evidence. In addition, the address of the parties recorded in the transaction contract can also be used as a basis for determining the location.

2.2.3 The Place Where the Contract Is Performed: Connecting Factor for Contract Disputes

In respect of contract disputes, in addition to the court of the place where the defendant is located, the court of the place where the contract is performed also has jurisdiction over such disputes. When determining the place of contract performance, we should first examine whether the contract has an agreement on the place of performance. If there is no agreement on the place of performance in the contract, the place of performance will be generally determined according to the subject matter in dispute. Common situations in practice are as follows:

(1) If the subject matter in dispute is to pay the price agreed in the contract, the place where the receiving party is located shall be the place of contract performance.

2.2 The Court of Which Place Has Jurisdiction—Territorial Jurisdiction ...

This means that the plaintiff has the right to bring a lawsuit with the court in its own place to recover the arrears under the contract.

(2) If the subject matter in dispute is the delivery of real estate, the place where the real estate is located shall be the place of contract performance.

(3) If the subject matter in dispute is other contents (such as delivery of goods, provision of services), the place where the party performing the obligation is located shall be the place of contract performance. This means that the plaintiff needs to file a lawsuit with the court at the defendant's location in order to require the defendant to perform its contractual obligations.

(4) In respect of the sales contract concluded through the information network (including the Internet, radio and television networks and other networks for transmitting information via electronic device), if the subject matter is delivered through the information network (such as providing software use license, playing streaming media video), the buyer's location shall be the place of contract performance; if the subject matter is delivered by other means (such as delivery of goods ordered online by express), the place of receipt shall be the place of contract performance.

There are special provisions in Chinese law on the place of performance of specific types of contracts such as insurance contracts and transportation contracts. We will not introduce them in detail here for the time being.

2.2.4 The Place Where the Infringement Is Committed and the Infringement Result Occurs: Connecting Factors for Infringement Disputes

In respect of infringement disputes, in addition to the court of the place where the defendant is located, the court of the place where the infringement is committed and the infringement result occurs also has jurisdiction over such disputes. Among them, for disputes arising from the use of information networks to publish infringing information (such as slandering competitors on the Internet, disseminating copyrighted movies without permission), the place where the infringement is committed includes the location of information equipment used to commit the infringement, and the place where the infringement result occurs include the location of the infringed. This means that the victims of information network infringement have the right to file lawsuits in their own location.

In respect of IP infringement cases, some right holder buys infringing products on the Internet, requires the seller to deliver the infringing products to a designated place, and then files a lawsuit with the court of the place of receipt. In the past, a considerable number of Chinese courts supported such a practice and held that the court at the place of receipt had jurisdiction over such cases. However, this practice allows the plaintiff to choose the competent court arbitrarily based on the place of receipt. The SPC, in a series of cases, pointed out that this practice not only unreasonably expanded the plaintiff's litigation rights but also unreasonably increased the defendant's suit response cost, which should not be supported. At present, most Chinese courts do not support the practice of filing an IP infringement lawsuit at the place of receipt. In contrast, it is more common and feasible to file lawsuits in the location of online shopping platform.

In addition, in terms of the infringement disputes caused by unqualified products and services, there are even more competent courts, specifically including the courts located in the following places:

(1) The place where the infringement is committed;
(2) The place where the infringement result occurs;
(3) The place where the defendant is located;
(4) The place of manufacture;
(5) The place of product sales; and
(6) The place of service provision.

2.2.5 The Place Where the Company Is Domiciled: Connecting Factor for Company-Related Organic Disputes

When trying disputes related to the incorporation, dissolution, capital reduction, resolution, change of registration items of a company and other organic issues, the court often needs to access the company's archives, financial and accounting vouchers, etc. In order to improve the trial efficiency of the court, Chinese law stipulates that these cases shall be uniformly under the jurisdiction of the court of the place where the company is domiciled, without considering other factors such as the location of the defendant.

It should be noted that the investment contract disputes between shareholders of a company are categorized as contract disputes, and the competent court shall be determined in accordance with the rules of contract disputes.

2.2.6 Prorogated Jurisdiction Rules

If the plaintiff brings a lawsuit with an incompetent court which has accepted the case, and other parties respond to the lawsuit and make defense without challenging the jurisdiction of the court, it shall be deemed that the said court has jurisdiction over the case.

However, if the plaintiff brings a lawsuit with such an incompetent court in violation of the provisions of hierarchical jurisdiction or exclusive jurisdiction, then the prorogated jurisdiction rules shall not be applied.

2.2.7 Exclusive Jurisdiction Rules

The term "exclusive jurisdiction cases" refers to such cases in which the parties are not allowed to choose the competent court by agreement and the prorogated jurisdiction rules are not applicable as well. For example, real right disputes arising from the right confirmation, division and neighboring relations of real estate shall be under the jurisdiction of the court of the place where the real estate is located. In addition, some contract disputes related to real estate (such as premises lease contract disputes and construction contract disputes) shall be also under the jurisdiction of the court where the real estate is located.

At present, the exclusive jurisdiction cases under the Chinese law include:

(1) Real estate disputes;
(2) Disputes arising from port operations;
(3) Disputes arising from inheritance;
(4) Disputes arising from the performance of the Sino-foreign equity joint venture contract in China;
(5) Disputes arising from the performance of the Sino-foreign contractual joint venture contract in China; and
(6) Disputes arising from the performance of the Sino-foreign cooperative exploration and development of natural resources contract in China.

As reflected by the CPL Revision Draft 2022, the scope of exclusive jurisdiction cases may expand to include (1) disputes arising from the incorporation, dissolution, liquidation, resolution and etc. of legal persons or non-legal person organizations incorporated in China; and (2) disputes arising from the validity of intellectual property rights that are examined and granted in China.

2.2.8 Cross-Region Centralized Jurisdiction of Specific Cases

In respect of some highly professional cases or cases with other special factors (such as the number of plaintiffs is large and they are scattered in different regions), the SPC or provincial high courts will designate some courts to exercise cross-region centralized jurisdiction in a certain region over certain types of cases, which would have been under the jurisdiction of a specific court in that certain region in accordance with the territorial jurisdiction rules. The originally competent courts will no longer have jurisdiction over such pertinent cases after they are subject to the cross-region centralized jurisdiction.

For example:

(1) All foreign-related first-instance commercial cases (not including financing-related cases) within Beijing Municipality shall be under the jurisdiction of the Fourth Intermediate People's Court of Beijing;

(2) First-instance civil and commercial cases such as securities issuance and fraud of enterprises listed on the START Market of Shanghai Stock Exchange shall be under the jurisdiction of the Shanghai Financial Court;
(3) First-instance invention and utility model patent cases in three southern cities of Jiangsu Province (i.e., Suzhou, Changzhou and Nantong) shall be under the jurisdiction of the Suzhou Intermediate People's Court;
(4) The first-instance civil cases about an investment product named "Yuan You Bao"[2] of Bank of China in Beijing, in which the relevant clients sued the head office and branches of Bank of China in Beijing, shall be under the centralized jurisdiction of Xicheng District Primary People's Court of Beijing and Beijing Second Intermediate People's Court respectively according to the amount in controversy.

2.2.9 Special Rules in Case of Foreign Parties as Defendants

Where the plaintiff brings a contract or property right lawsuit against a foreign party that has no domicile in China, even if the connecting factors under the general jurisdiction rules are not in China, the plaintiff also has the right to bring a lawsuit with the courts of China at the following places:

(1) The place where the contract is signed;
(2) The place where the contract is performed;
(3) The place where the subject matter is located;
(4) The place where the defendant's property available for seizure is located; and
(5) The place where the defendant's permanent representative office in China is located.

As reflected by the CPL Revision Draft 2022, the application scope of above rules is likely to expand to cover non-property right lawsuit and other disputes that have appropriate connection with China. Correspondingly, the place where the infringement is committed, the place where the infringement result occurs and other appropriate places may become connecting factors for the Chinese court's jurisdiction. A specific example is Chinese consumer may bring lawsuit against foreign business operators or their branches without domicile in China at the place where the consumer is located.

It should be noted that although the permanent representative office of a foreign enterprise in China is registered in China, it neither enjoys the standing of a legal person nor can it engage in profit-making activities. Some Chinese courts held that given the operation funds of such representative offices came from foreign enterprises, and they were not organizations having their own property, they were not

---

[2] "Yuan You Bao" is a financial product launched by the Bank of China investing in futures contracts in the international crude oil market. Given that the May contract for US-based WTI crude oil futures printed a negative settlement price on 20 April 2020, many investors suffered great losses and therefore filed claims against Bank of China on the ground that it was responsible for the losses.

qualified for litigation in China. Therefore, if a representative office is involved in litigation in China, the Chinese court may list the pertinent foreign enterprise as a litigant and order it to be ultimately responsible for the enforcement of judgment.

(Reference provisions and information for Sect. 2.2).[3]

2.3 Objection to Jurisdiction and Case Transferring

2.3.1 The Defendant May Raise an Objection to Jurisdiction

If the defendant considers that the court accepting the case has no jurisdiction, it may raise an objection with the court accepting the case within 15 days (or 30 days if the defendant has no domicile within the territory of China) as of the date of receiving the statement of claim. If the objection is tenable, the court accepting the case will make a ruling to transfer the case to the competent court for trial; if the objection is untenable, the court accepting the case will overrule the objection. The party dissatisfied with the ruling may appeal and request the higher court to render a final ruling.

Chinese law does not restrict the party's right to object to jurisdiction or file an appeal; besides, the cost of filing jurisdiction objections and appeals is pretty low. However, it takes time for the court to make a ruling. If either party appeals, the first-instance court needs to sort out the files and transfer them to the second-instance

---

[3] *CPL (Revised in 2021): Article 22, 24, 27, 29, 34–36, 131, 272, 273.*

CPL Revision Draft 2022: Article 276, 279, 280.

Judicial Interpretation of CPL (Revised in 2022): Article 3, 4, 18, 20, 22, 24–26, 29, 30, 529.

Provisions of Beijing High People's Court on the Case Jurisdiction of Beijing Fourth Intermediate People's Court (Revised in 2018).

《北京市高级人民法院关于北京市第四中级人民法院案件管辖的规定》(2018年修订).

Notice of the Supreme People's Court on Printing and Distributing Several Opinions on Providing Judicial Protection for the Establishment of STAR Market and the Pilot Reform of Registration System (Fa Fa [2019] No.17).

《最高人民法院印发＜关于为设立科创板并试点注册制改革提供司法保障的若干意见＞的通知》(法发〔2019〕17号).

Reply of the Supreme People's Court on Approving the Establishment of Specialized Trial Divisions Within and the Cross-region Jurisdiction over Some Intellectual Property Cases by Intermediate People's Courts of Nanjing, Suzhou, Wuhan and Chengdu (Fa [2017] No. 2).

《最高人民法院关于同意南京市、苏州市、武汉市、成都市中级人民法院内设专门审判机构并跨区域管辖部分知识产权案件的批复》(法〔2017〕2号).

Notice of Jiangsu Province High People's Court on Design Patent Cases and Non-technical Intellectual Property Cases with a Disputed Amount of More Than RMB 3 Million under the Jurisdiction of Wuxi Intermediate People's Court, etc.

《江苏省高级人民法院关于由无锡市中级人民法院等管辖外观设计专利案件以及300万元以上非技术类知识产权案件的通知》.

Announcement of Beijing High People's Court on Centralized Jurisdiction over Civil Litigation Cases Concerning an Investment Product Named "Yuan You Bao" of Bank of China.

《北京市高级人民法院关于涉中国银行"原油宝"事件民事诉讼案件集中管辖的公告》.

court, which, after making a final ruling, also needs to transfer the case files back to the first-instance court, which will then continue to hear the substantive issues of the case. Therefore, some defendants will raise objections to jurisdiction without any justified reason to maliciously delay the proceedings.

In order to tackle the abuse of the right of objection, Chinese courts are speeding up the examination of jurisdiction objection, trying to simplify the trial process and document preparation requirements of jurisdiction objection, thus reducing the possibility of abusing the right of objection. At the same time, some courts try to impose disciplinary sanctions such as admonition and fine on the parties who obviously abuse the right of objection. We believe that the abuse of the right of objection can be solved gradually.

2.3.2 The Court May also Examine the Jurisdiction Issue Ex Officio

Although the defendant does not raise any objection to jurisdiction, a court may still examine its jurisdiction over the case ex officio. If the court finds that it has no jurisdiction, it will make a ruling to transfer the case to the competent court for trial. Different from the defendant's objection to jurisdiction, the parties have no right to appeal the transfer decision made by the court on its own initiative.

2.3.3 Case Transferring

The court, after making the case transferring decision, will transfer all the case files to a new court. Although the court accepting the transferred case considers that it does not have jurisdiction, it still cannot re-transfer the case to other courts, and in this situation, it must report to a higher court for determining the jurisdiction. This is to prevent the courts from buck-passing and damaging the litigation rights of the parties.

(Reference provisions and information for Sect. 2.3).[4]

---

[4] *CPL (Revised in 2021): Article 37, 131, 157.*

Open Access This chapter is licensed under the terms of the Creative Commons Attribution 4.0 International License (http://creativecommons.org/licenses/by/4.0/), which permits use, sharing, adaptation, distribution and reproduction in any medium or format, as long as you give appropriate credit to the original author(s) and the source, provide a link to the Creative Commons license and indicate if changes were made.

The images or other third party material in this chapter are included in the chapter's Creative Commons license, unless indicated otherwise in a credit line to the material. If material is not included in the chapter's Creative Commons license and your intended use is not permitted by statutory regulation or exceeds the permitted use, you will need to obtain permission directly from the copyright holder.

Chapter 3
Case Filing and Determination of the Adjudicatory Personnel

Abstract After determining the competent court, the plaintiff can bring the lawsuit by submitting the statement of claim, necessary evidence, and other formality documents to the court. However, it is noteworthy that foreign parties, especially foreign companies and other institutions, need to prepare a series of formality documents as required by the Chinese court to participate in litigation, which can sometimes be somewhat cumbersome. Therefore, it is necessary to spare sufficient time to get ready. Upon receipt of the plaintiff's materials, the Chinese court shall examine them to limited extent, and file the case upon satisfaction of certain statutory conditions. To facilitate foreign parties to submit filing materials online, the SPC establishes an Internet platform for foreign parties and streamlines the case-filing procedures from several aspects. Due to some concerns, however, we would advise that foreign organizations prepare paper materials in the traditional way, and seek help from Chinese lawyers for case filing. After the case filing, Chinese courts generally determine the judge(s) for a case through the computer-based random allocation, but under special circumstances, Chinese courts will directly appoint the judge(s) for a case. There is no jury system in China, and the facts and legal issues involved in the case should be decided by the collegial panel or the sole judge. Nevertheless, Chinese citizens can participate in the trial by joining the collegial panel as people's assessors. The power of people's assessors is generally the same as that of judges, but in some cases, they only have the right to vote on the finding of facts.

3.1 Preparations Before Bringing a Lawsuit—Formality Documents for Foreign Parties

3.1.1 Certificates of Subject Qualification—"Who Am I" and "Who Represents Me"

To participate in China's civil litigation, foreign natural persons need to submit passports or other equivalents proving their identities as certificates of subject qualification.

As to foreign companies and other institutions, the certificates of subject qualification are more complex, which include:

(1) Business license, or the certificate document on good standing issued by enterprise registration authority;
(2) Documents certifying the status of the legal representative or the authorized representative (e.g. the company's bylaws, resolution of the board of directors, and etc.);
(3) Documents certifying the identity ("identity certificate") of the legal representative or the authorized representative, including his/her name and position; and
(4) Passport or other identity documents of the legal representative or the authorized representative.

The above documents mainly concern 'legal representative' (法定代表人) and 'authorized representative' (授权代表人), so it is necessary to clarify these two concepts. Chinese companies or foreign companies all need a natural person, on behalf of the company, to sign the litigation documents and to participate in litigation. Each Chinese company has a registered 'legal representative', who is entitled to represent the company to participate in litigation without the need for additional authorization. If a foreign company has a legal representative, he or she may also participate in the litigation on behalf of the company. In order to certify his or her status, the foreign company generally needs to submit its bylaws or other similar documents. As for the foreign company without a legal representative, it is required to specifically empower an 'authorized representative' to participate in the lawsuit. In this respect, the foreign company needs to submit a related board resolution made pursuant to its bylaws.

It is noteworthy that Chinese courts also require an "identity certificate" of the legal representative or the authorized representative. This certificate generally contains only a single sentence, such as 'A certain person holds a certain position in the company, he/she is also the legal representative/the authorized representative of that company'. This may seem superfluous; however, such simple, repetitive documents must not be omitted.

The above materials should be signed by the directors or the secretary of the company, etc., according to the foreign local law and the company bylaws. It should be noted that China emphasizes great importance to the seal. Therefore, it is recommended that foreign companies affix their seals on all the documents, even if these seals are merely decorative and not legally effective in their own country.

3.1.2 Power of Attorney—"Who Is My Lawyer"

To participate in litigation in Chinese courts, foreign companies often need to appoint Chinese lawyers, and hence need to submit the power of attorney to the courts.

3.1 Preparations Before Bringing a Lawsuit—Formality Documents … 41

The power of attorney shall be signed by the legal representative or the authorized representative as described above, and preferably stamped with the company seal.

If the company does not mandate a lawyer, then the legal representative or the authorized representative need to participate in the litigation in person.

3.1.3 Notarization and Authentication—"My Documents Are Authentic"

In addition to the requirements on content, Chinese courts also require the formality documents be notarized, authenticated and translated. Understanding the purpose of such requirements will be helpful to prepare documents correctly.

3.1.3.1 What Are Notarization and Authentication

Most of the subject qualification documents and the authorization procedures of foreign companies are formed outside the territory of China. In order to confirm the authenticity of these materials, Chinese laws require that the content and the formation process of the materials be notarized by a local foreign notary (the step of "notarization"), and then be authenticated by the Chinese embassy or consulate in that country so as to certify that the signature or seal of the notary is true (the step of "authentication"). Only then can the materials become effective.

In practice, the steps of notarization and authentication are usually as below:

(1) "Notarization" by a local foreign notary;
(2) Certification by foreign government officers that the identity and signature of the notary are authentic; and
(3) "Authentication" by the Chinese embassy or consulate in that country that the identity and signature of foreign government officers are authentic. The attached picture above is a sample of the Chinese Embassy and Consulate's authentication documents. It only certifies that "Both the seal of the United States Department of the State, and the signature of the assistant authentication officer CHANA

TURNER in the previous documents are authentic"; and the authority that issued the instruments should be responsible for their content.

If China has entered into a treaty with a certain country, then the certification process should be carried out in accordance with the treaty.

3.1.3.2 The Content of Notarization

As introduced previously, "authentication" is merely for certifying that the signature or seal of the notary is true, while "notarization" is the key to certify the authenticity of the documents. According to our experience, the notarized letter must at least indicate the following content.

(1) The business license or the certificate document on good standing: (a) the time and place of obtaining the copies; and (b) the copies are consistent with the original;
(2) The company bylaws: (a) the time and place of obtaining the copies; and (b) the copies are consistent with the original;
(3) The resolution of the board of directors: (a) the time and place of the resolution; and (b) the signature and seal are carried out under the witness of the notary, which are authentic and effective;
(4) The "identity certificate": (a) the time and place to sign the certificate; and (b) the signature and seal are carried out under the witness of the notary, which are authentic and effective;
(5) The passport or other identity documents: the documents are authentic and effective; and

(6) The power of attorney: (a) the time and place to sign the power of attorney; and (b) the signature and seal are carried out under the witness of the notary, which are authentic and effective.

3.1.4 Translation

All materials in foreign languages submitted to Chinese courts should be accompanied by Chinese translation (except for the cases trialed by the China International Commercial Court of the SPC). In practice, some Chinese courts even require that the translation be provided by the appointed translation agencies.

(Reference provisions and information for Sect. 3.1).[1]

3.2 Bringing a Lawsuit and Case Filing

3.2.1 General Process of Case Filing

The plaintiff may submit the statement of claim either personally at the court, or by mail as allowed by some Chinese courts. In addition, Chinese courts have established online case filing platforms (including WeChat, the most popular social media in China). These channels greatly facilitate the parties to bring a lawsuit.

The court, upon receipt of the statement of claim, will examine the same and decide whether to file a case. For quite a long time, Chinese courts adopted the "case filing examination system (立案审查制)", that is, before the case filing, the court can examine substantive issues such as the qualification of the parties, the facts and the legal relations on which the action is based, and then decide whether to file a case. This approach grants the court considerable discretion in terms of the case filing. Some courts refuse to file a case for the parties out of various unjustified reasons, which damages the litigation rights of the parties.

In order to tackle the "difficulty in case filing", the Supreme People's Court has made reform since 1 May 2015, changing the "case filing examination system" to the "case filing registration system". As required by the reform, the court shall receive and examine the statement of claim submitted by the plaintiff on the spot. The court shall, upon examination of the statement of claim and satisfaction of the following conditions, file and register the case on the spot; if the satisfaction of legal conditions cannot be determined on the spot, the court is still required to make a decision on the case filing within 7 days:

(1) The plaintiff has a direct interest in the case;
(2) There is a known defendant;

---

[1] *CPL (Revised in 2021): Article 51, 269, 271.*
 Judicial Interpretation of CPL (Revised in 2022): Article 521, 522, 525.

(3) There are specific claims, facts and reasons;
(4) The subject matter is a civil dispute acceptable by the court, and the court has jurisdiction over the case; and
(5) The action is not prohibited by the law due to endangering national sovereignty and territorial integrity, and the like.

After the reform of the case filing system, the "difficulty in case filing" has been effectively alleviated. Nevertheless, for more complex and foreign-related cases, judges may raise a series of questions when examining the statement of claim. Some judges may still examine the substantive issues of the case due to their previous working habits. Therefore, the on-site statement of claim submission can better facilitate communication with judges, and improve the case filing efficiency of complex cases in particular.

The court will, after the case filing, notify the plaintiff to pay the court costs (for court costs, see Sect. 1.5), and allocate the case to the corresponding tribunal and the specific case handling judge(s) according to the cause of action (for cause of action, see Sect. 1.4).

In practice, in order to alleviate the pressure brought by the litigation explosion, some courts that accept a large number of cases will first conduct a mediation after receiving the statement of claim. If the mediation fails, the court will then ordinarily file the case (for pre-trial mediation, see Sect. 11.2).

3.2.2 Cross-Border Online Case Filing—Latest Facilitation Measures for Foreign Parties

Nowadays, online case filing has been made available in many Chinese courts. But most case-filing platforms provide services only in the Chinese language. Before using such services, users are required to go through real-name authentication, which relies on China's identity card system. Therefore, such online case-filing platforms are almost only useful for Chinese parties. If foreign parties need to file cases through the Internet, usually they need to hire a Chinese lawyer on their behalf.

On 3 February 2021, to facilitate foreign parties to submit filing materials directly, the SPC issued the Several Provisions of the Supreme People's Court on Providing Online Case-filing Services for Foreign Litigants (最高人民法院关于为跨境诉讼当事人提供网上立案服务的若干规定), which provides an Internet platform for foreign parties to file cases with Chinese courts and streamlines the case-filing procedures from several aspects.

3.2.2.1 Case Filing Through the Mobile App

The online case-filing platform operated by the SPC for foreign parties is called "People's Court Online Service", an applet embedded in WeChat (China's largest mobile social media). Therefore, if you want to use People's Court Online Service to file a case, you must install WeChat first. And after that, a foreign party can, theoretically, file a case with a mobile phone.

3.2.2.2 Streamline of the Identity Verification

When filing a case online for the first time, Chinese courts need to verify the identity of the parties. According to the new rules, Chinese courts can verify the identity of the parties through the information retained in the identity verification platform of China's National Immigration Administration. That is, for the parties who have entry-exit record in China, the procedure of identity verification will be simplified.

If the verification cannot be done by this method, Chinese courts can also conduct manual verification on the identity materials provided by the parties online. For the specific materials to be provided, please refer to Sect. 4.1.

Although online verification does not require the parties to provide the paper originals to the court, the notarization, the authentication and other procedures are still needed.

3.2.2.3 Streamline of the Power of Attorney

Under the new rules, foreign parties can apply to Chinese courts for "online video witness", i.e., under the witness of the judge, the party (and his/her interpreter) and the lawyer online at the same time, the party may sign the power of attorney for entrusting Chinese lawyer. If this method is adopted, there is no need for notarization, authentication and other cumbersome procedures.

3.2.2.4 Actual Operation

On the second day after the promulgation of the new rules, a Japanese citizen signed the power of attorney for entrusting Chinese lawyers through online video witness, thus completing the cross-border case filing with Fengxian Primary People's Court of Shanghai Municipality. In addition, this platform also provides services to residents of Hong Kong, Macau and Taiwan, as well as Mainland Chinese citizens living abroad.

At present, courts in Beijing and Shanghai have already helped several overseas mainland Chinese citizens and Taiwan residents complete cross-border case filing.

3.2.2.5 Our Observation and Suggestion

According to the news disclosed so far, most of the parties using the cross-border case filing platform are natural persons who can speak Chinese. In the future, with the further improvement of the platform functions, we believe that the platform can provide convenience for more foreign parties.

At the same time, we have noticed that there are still some obstacles for foreign companies or organizations to use this platform.

First of all, regarding identity verification, China's entry-exit system only retains the information of natural persons, and therefore foreign companies/organizations still need to prepare materials and go through notarization and authentication procedures in the traditional way for identity verification, but no paper originals are required now.

Second, if foreign companies/organizations want to simplify the procedures for entrusting Chinese lawyers, they need to designate representatives to participate in video witness, and such representatives are, in principle, required to hold notarized and authenticated POAs, which in fact causes more troubles for the parties.

In view of the above problems and questions frequently raised by judges during the filing of foreign-related cases, we would advise that foreign organizations prepare paper materials in the traditional way, and hire Chinese lawyers for case filing with the court offline. Chinese lawyers can also use their own accounts to file cases online if their foreign clients are in a tight schedule.

Generally speaking, we believe that it will be more and more convenient for foreign parties to participate in litigation in China. However, to avoid technical, communication, and other problems in case filing, it is still highly necessary to hire Chinese lawyers.

(Reference provisions and information for Sect. 3.2).[2]

3.3 Determining the Adjudicatory Personnel

3.3.1 The Composition of Collegial Panel

After a case is filed, the Chinese court will determine the collegial panel of the case. The collegial panel for first-instance cases under ordinary procedures is generally composed of three persons. For complex and major cases, Chinese courts may increase the number of the panel members, *provided, however, that* the number of the panel members must be an odd number.

When determining the judges for a specific case, the Chinese court mostly use computer programs to randomly assign judges of the corresponding tribunal for the

---

[2] *CPL (Revised in 2021): Article 122.*

Provisions of the Supreme People's Court on Several Issues Concerning Acceptance and Registration of Cases by People's Courts (Fa Shi [2015] No.8): Article 2, 8.

《最高人民法院关于人民法院登记立案若干问题的规定》(法释〔2015〕8号).

Several Provisions of the Supreme People's Court on Providing Online Case-filing Services for Foreign Litigants.

《最高人民法院关于为跨境诉讼当事人提供网上立案服务的若干规定》

3.3 Determining the Adjudicatory Personnel

case. In a few cases (such as multiple cases with the same defendant and similar circumstances), the court may appoint judges directly.

There will be one undertaking judge among the members of the collegial panel. The undertaking judge is responsible for promoting the pre-trial preparations, examining the evidence, assisting the presiding judge in organizing the court trial, drafting the judgment and etc. Because of the above responsibilities, the undertaking judge is often the person who understands the case to the greatest extent. The opinion of the undertaking judge plays a critical and even decisive role in the case trial.

For purposes such as enhancing judicial credibility, China allows eligible citizens to participate in the trial as people's assessors. Therefore, the collegial panel can be composed entirely of judges, or judges and people's assessors. Generally, people's assessors are randomly selected from permanent residents who have reached the age of 28 within the jurisdiction of the court, but those of specific occupations (including procurator, police, lawyer, etc.) cannot serve as people's assessors. According to the Chinese law, people's assessors enjoy the same rights, including the right to vote when evaluating cases, as judges in most cases. In terms of public interest litigation (for public interest litigation, see Chap. 8) and other influential cases, people's assessors only have the right to vote on the finding of facts but not the application of law.

In addition, in order to cope with the rapid quantity growth of cases, Chinese law stipulates that when the primary courts try cases with clear-cut facts and rights and obligations, even if the ordinary procedure is applied, they can be tried by one judge like cases under summary procedure (for summary procedure, see Sect. 5.6).

3.3.2 No Jury in China—What Is People's Assessor

3.3.2.1 Powers and Duties of People's Assessor

Although there is no jury system in China, Chinese citizens can participate in the trial by joining the collegial panel as people's assessors. In most cases, the power of people's assessor is the same as that of judges. During the court trial, people's assessors may question the parties. During the after-trial deliberation, people's assessors have the right to express their opinions and enjoy the same voting right as judges. However, in the following cases tried by the seven-member collegial panel, people's assessors only have the right to vote on the finding of facts, excluding the application of law.

The people's assessor system bears a good original intention. However, in practice, it gets criticized from time to time for being a trumpery, that is, people's assessors only appear in court in a symbolic sense without expressing any opinion during the trial and the after-trial deliberation, and the case trial is completely dominated by judges.

To change this awkward situation, the SPC has formulated a series of systems to help people's assessors better perform their duties. For example, people's assessors may question the parties involved in the trial, and the presiding judge can guide people's assessors to ask questions around the disputed issues; during the case deliberation by the collegial panel, the undertaking judge will first introduce relevant laws and evidence rules involved in the case to people's assessors who will then give their opinions, and other judges and the presiding judge will give their opinions at last. We hope that these systems will make a better use of the people's assessor system.

3.3.2.2 What Civil Cases Can people's Assessor Participate In

Firstly, people's assessors can participate in the first-instance trial only, excluding the second-instance trial (for China's hierarchical trial system, see Sect. 1.2).

Secondly, it is up to the court to decide in which civil cases people's assessors may participate. However, unless otherwise provided by law, people's assessors should be invited to participate in the trial of the following cases:

(1) Cases involving group interests and/or public interests;
(2) Cases of widespread concern to the people or with great social influence; and
(3) Cases whose circumstances are complex or special that require the participation of people's assessors in the trial.

Thirdly, for ordinary civil cases in which people's assessors participate in the trial, the collegial panel is composed of 3 members, including 1–2 people's assessors. However, for the following special civil cases, the collegial panel is composed of 7 members, including 4 people's assessors:

(1) Cases of public interest litigation (for public interest litigation, see Chap. 8);
(2) Cases with great social influence of land acquisition and demolition, ecological environment protection, and food and drug safety; and
(3) Other cases with great social influence.

Fourthly, people's assessors should not participate in the trial of special types of cases, such as cases under special procedure, cases of recognizing and enforcing foreign divorce judgments.

3.3.2.3 Who Can Be people's Assessor?

People's assessors must be Chinese citizens over the age of 28. Under normal circumstances, people's assessors should be high school graduates or above and are physically capable of performing their duties normally.

One of the important purposes of the people's assessor system is to let laypersons participate in and/or supervise judicial activities. For this reason, the following persons engaged in law related occupations cannot serve as people's assessors:

(1) Members of the standing committee of the people's congress and staff of the supervisory committee, the people's court, the people's procuratorate, the public security organ, the state security organ and the judicial administrative organ;

3.3 Determining the Adjudicatory Personnel

(2) Lawyers, notaries, arbitrators and grass-roots legal service workers; and
(3) Other persons who are not suitable to serve as people's assessors due to their occupations.

In addition, people's assessors must also support the P.R.C. Constitution, abide by law and discipline, and be decent and impartial. For this reason, people who have been subject to criminal punishment, who are dishonest judgment debtors (for dishonest judgment debtors, see Sect. 10.5) and who have violated law and discipline cannot serve as people's assessors.

3.3.2.4 How Does the Court Select people's Assessor

When people's assessors are needed for the case trial, the court will randomly select candidates from the roster of people's assessors which is also prepared mainly by random selection. The court will, in concert with the administrative organ, first randomly select five times the number of candidates from the permanent residents in the jurisdiction of the court, and then randomly select people's assessors from the qualified candidates who are willing to serve as people's assessors. In addition, citizens themselves can also serve as people's assessors through voluntary application or recommendation by employers and other institutions.

The term of office of the people's assessors is five years, and generally they may not be re-elected.

To determine the people's assessors of a specific case, the court shall randomly select people's assessors from the roster of people's assessors 7 days before the court trial. The court may also select a certain number of alternate people's assessors and determine the order of alternation. If specific types of cases (such as intellectual property cases) require people's assessors with expertise, the court can randomly select and determine the candidates from the qualified people's assessors.

(Reference provisions and information for Sect. 3.3).[3]

---

[3] *CPL (Revised in 2021): Article 39, 40, 122.*

People's Assessor Law of the People's Republic of China (Promulgated in 2018): Article 5, 6, 9–11, 13, 15, 16, 19, 21, 22.

《中华人民共和国人民陪审员法》(2018年颁布).

Provisions of the Supreme People's Court on Further Strengthening Duties of Collegial Panel (Fa Shi [2010] No.1): Article 3.

《最高人民法院关于进一步加强合议庭职责的若干规定》(法释〔2010〕1号).

Notice of the Supreme People's Court on Printing and Distributing the Code of Conduct for Judges (Fa Fa [2010] No. 54): Article 47.

《最高人民法院关于印发 < 法官行为规范 > 的通知》(法发〔2010〕54号).

Opinions of the Supreme People's Court on Regulating the Working System of Collegial Panel (Fa Fa [2022] No.31).

最高人民法院关于规范合议庭运行机制的意见(法发〔2022〕31号).

Interpretation of the Supreme People's Court on Several Issues of Application of the People's Assessor Law of the People's Republic of China (Fa Shi [2019] No.5): Article 3, 5, 11, 12.

《最高人民法院关于适用 < 中华人民共和国人民陪审员法 > 若干问题的解释》(法释〔2019〕5号).

Open Access This chapter is licensed under the terms of the Creative Commons Attribution 4.0 International License (http://creativecommons.org/licenses/by/4.0/), which permits use, sharing, adaptation, distribution and reproduction in any medium or format, as long as you give appropriate credit to the original author(s) and the source, provide a link to the Creative Commons license and indicate if changes were made.

The images or other third party material in this chapter are included in the chapter's Creative Commons license, unless indicated otherwise in a credit line to the material. If material is not included in the chapter's Creative Commons license and your intended use is not permitted by statutory regulation or exceeds the permitted use, you will need to obtain permission directly from the copyright holder.

Chapter 4
Service of Court Documents

Abstract The court documents will be served after the determination of adjudicatory personnel. In China, the service of court documents is effected by the court, with necessary assistance from the party if needed. Chinese courts may serve court documents by personal service, service by mail and the like. In practice, service by mail is the preferred method of service among most Chinese courts. However, to improve the efficiency of service, Chinese courts are now actively trying electronic service. If court documents cannot be served by the foregoing means, the court may also resort to service by publication. Due to fast and widespread population migration and intentional evasion of the service of court documents, Chinese courts are facing "difficulty in effecting service of court documents" to a certain extent, which in turn upsets the litigation efficiency. To solve this problem, Chinese courts have taken various measures, which significantly improve the efficiency of service. If the defendant is a foreign party without domicile in China, the Chinese court may serve court documents on its designated personnel or organization in China. In the absence of such personnel or organization, Chinese courts usually serve court documents in accordance with international treaties such as the Convention on the Service Abroad of Judicial and Extrajudicial Documents in Civil or Commercial Matters (hereinafter referred to as the "Hague Service Convention"). To the extent permitted by the internal law of the state of the person to be served, Chinese courts may also serve court documents by mail and electronic means. Anyway, service by publication still remains the last resort for service of court documents of Chinese courts. As a contracting state to the Hague Service Convention, China is obligated to assist foreign courts in service of court documents in accordance therewith. For this purpose, Chinese courts have also stipulated a clear process for assisting foreign courts in service of court documents. If there are bilateral treaties between China and other contracting states to the Hague Service Convention, there will be some flexibilities in the application of either the Hague Service Convention or bilateral treaties.

4.1 Basic Methods for Service of Court Documents in China

4.1.1 Personal Service

The court staff may serve court documents directly to the person to be served or the designated agent for acceptance of service, attorney or an adult family member living with the said person. If the person to be served is an organization, the court may serve court documents on its legal representative or person in charge or on its mailroom clerk. In practice, in case of personal service, the person to be served or the designated agent for acceptance of service is usually served in court.

4.1.2 Service by Leaving Rejected Court Documents at the Domicile

Where the person to be served rejects court documents, the court staff may leave the same at the domicile of the said person and record such situation by photography and/or video, or by inviting others (generally representatives of the neighborhood committee of the said person's domicile or representatives of the said person's employer) to witness such situation and then sign for confirmation.

4.1.3 Service by Mail

The court may serve court documents by mail through nationally recognized postal agencies, and court documents will be deemed duly served upon signature by the person to be served or the aforesaid persons with the power of accepting personal service. Both the court and the parties can query the mail delivery status through the Internet.

In practice, limited by manpower, it is difficult for Chinese courts to serve court documents by personal service and service by leaving rejected court documents at the domicile on a large scale. Therefore, service by mail is the preferred method of service among most Chinese courts. Thus, the mailing address of the parties is critical to the integrity of the legal proceedings. For this purpose, the Chinese court will, at the time of case filing, generally require the plaintiff to provide the defendant's address to its knowledge and fill in the service address confirmation form. Once the defendant is successfully contacted, the Chinese court will also require the defendant to fill in the service address confirmation form immediately.

4.1.4 Electronic Service

With the consent of the person to be served, Chinese courts may serve court documents by electronic means such as fax, e-mail, SMS, social media (such as WeChat). In practice, Chinese courts will generally require the parties to indicate their consent to electronic service in the service address confirmation form, and fill in the address for electronic service.

4.1.5 Service by Publication

If the whereabouts of the person to be served are unknown or the service by other methods cannot be effected, the court will serve court documents by publication. The service will be deemed effected 30 days after the publication. The publication may be posted on the bulletin board of the court or on the domicile of the person to be served, or published in the People's Court Daily (人民法院报, a newspaper sponsored by the SPC) or on the Internet.

At present, the publication is generally made in the People's Court Daily and the People's Court Announcement (available at: https://rmfygg.court.gov.cn/) or other judicial websites set up by local courts. In the future, Chinese courts will establish a unified electronic judicial publication platform, and most publications will be made through the Internet.

It should be noted that the court can only serve court documents by publication provided that it has exhausted other methods for service of court documents. If the parties' right to due process is damaged due to the court's failure to exhaust other methods for service of court documents, the parties not duly served may appeal on this ground.

The expenses incurred by service by publication via the People's Court Daily will generally depend on the type and urgency of the publication. Generally, the expenses for the publication of statement of claim and summons are RMB 260, generally to be borne by the plaintiff.

(Reference provisions and information for Sect. 4.1).[1]

---

[1] *CPL (Revised in 2021): Article 88–91, 95.*
  Judicial Interpretation of CPL (Revised in 2022): Article 130, 131, 135, 136, 138.
  Measures for the Payment of Litigation Fees: Article 12.
  《诉讼费用交纳办法》

4.2 How to Tackle "Difficulty in Effecting Service of Court Documents"

With the development of economy and society, China's population and enterprise migration is speeding up. Many natural persons reside in places different from their registered domicile, and so do many enterprises. In addition, after being informed of the lawsuit, some parties evade the service of court documents by providing false addresses and/or refusing to be served, so as to delay the legal proceedings. For such reasons, Chinese courts are facing "difficulty in effecting service of court documents" to a certain extent, which in turn upsets the litigation efficiency. Chinese courts have therefore taken various measures, which significantly improve the efficiency of service.

4.2.1 Reform Measures for "Difficulty in Effecting Service of Court Documents" on Enterprises

In order to improve the efficiency of service by mail, the courts in Beijing and Shanghai have cooperated with the local enterprise registration authorities to include the service address of an enterprise as a registration item of the enterprise file. Before the person to be served fill in the service address confirmation form, the court may effect the service of court documents by mailing to the registered service address.

4.2.2 Vigorously Promote Electronic Service

Given that electronic service is more convenient than service by traditional methods, courts across China are now vigorously promoting electronic service. For example, the High People's Court of Guangdong Province cooperates with Netease to provide, free of charge, the parties and the lawyers with special e-mail for electronic service. The High People's Court of Shandong Province stipulates that for cases tried by primary courts, if the parties entrust their lawyers with the service of court documents, electronic service shall be used preferably.

4.2.3 Combat Service Evasion

In addition to the foregoing reform measures, pursuant to the Notice of the Supreme People's Court on Printing and Distributing Several Opinions on Further Strengthening Service of Court Documents in Civil Matters (hereinafter referred to as the "Guiding Opinions") promulgated in July 2017, if the person to be served refuses to

4.2 How to Tackle "Difficulty in Effecting Service of Court Documents"

confirm the service address, or evades service by refusing to respond to the lawsuit, answer the phone, avoiding court documents server, moving away from the original residence, etc., the court may take the following address as the service address:

(1) The service address agreed by the parties in the contract and/or correspondence involved in the lawsuit;
(2) The address specified in the written documents submitted by the person to be served in case of no agreed service address;
(3) The address provided by the person to be served in other litigation and/or arbitration cases in the past one year if the foregoing two situations are not applicable;
(4) The address frequently used by the person to be served in civil activities in the past one year if the foregoing three situations are not applicable. To our knowledge, some courts believe that the address commonly used by the person to be served for online shopping and ordering takeout can be taken as the service address; and
(5) If it is still unable to determine the service address according to the foregoing provisions, the registered domicile or the registered habitual residence, in case of a natural person, and the legally registered/filed domicile, in case of an organization, shall be taken as the service address.

More importantly, the Guiding Opinions also provides that if the person to be served fails to receive court documents due to its provision of inaccurate service address or refusal to provide service address, the service of court documents shall be deemed effected when the court leaves court documents at the service address or when court documents are returned to the court by the postal agency. Although in practice, the application of this provision remains to be strengthened, it sheds us some light on tackling "difficulty in effecting service of court documents". We hope that legislators will sufficiently consider the above opinions at the next revision of the CPL.

(Reference provisions and information for Sect. 4.2).[2]

---

[2] *CPL (Revised in 2021): Article 90.*

The Notice of the Supreme People's Court on Printing and Distributing Several Opinions on Further Strengthening Service of Court Documents in Civil Matters (Fa Fa [2017] No.19): Article 7, 8.

《最高人民法院印发＜关于进一步加强民事送达工作的若干意见＞的通知》(法发〔2017〕19号).

Implementation Opinions of Beijing High People's Court and Beijing Municipal Bureau of Market Supervision and Administration on Promoting the Confirmation of Addresses for Service of Legal Process of Enterprises and Other Market Players (For Trial Implementation) (8 April 2020).

《北京市高级人民法院、北京市市场监督管理局关于推进企业等市场主体法律文书送达地址承诺确认工作的实施意见(试行)》(2020年4月8日).

Implementation Opinions of Shanghai High People's Court and Shanghai Municipal Bureau of Market Supervision and Administration on Confirmation of Addresses for Service of Legal Process and Commitment of Assuming Corresponding Responsibilities (For Trial Implementation) (Hu Gao Fa [2020] No.41).

4.3 How to Serve Court Documents on Foreign Parties Without Domicile in China

4.3.1 Service on Personnel or Organizations in China

For a foreign party without domicile in China, the Chinese court may, according to the methods for service of court documents in China, serve court documents on its following personnel or organizations in China:

(1) The representative or primary person in charge (including director, supervisor, senior manager, etc.);
(2) The representative office (generally refers to the representative office established under the Chinese law);
(3) The branch authorized by the party to be served;
(4) The business agent authorized by the party to be served; and
(5) The litigation representative (unless otherwise prohibited by the power of attorney).

Besides, if a foreign natural person establishes a wholly foreign-owned enterprise in China or holds the position such as legal representative and/or director of an enterprise in China, the Chinese court may serve court documents on such enterprise which will then forward the relevant documents to the foreign natural person. The Chinese court may also serve court documents on an adult family member living with the foreign natural person to be served in China. However, the service through such approaches can only be deemed effected upon acknowledgment of the receipt by the person to be served.

As reflected by the CPL Revision Draft 2022, the Chinese court is likely to further expand methods of service on foreign parties' personnel or organizations in China, and cancel the above requirement on acknowledgement of the receipt by the person to be served applicable to certain service approaches.

If the foregoing conditions are not fulfilled, Chinese courts may serve court documents through the following ways:

《上海市高级人民法院、上海市市场监督管理局关于企业确认诉讼文书送达地址并承诺相应责任的实施意见 (试行) 》(沪高法〔2020〕41号).

Notice of Shandong Province High People's Court on Printing and Distributing the Handling Process of Civil and Commercial Cases by Primary People's Courts (Lu Gao Fa [2019] No. 59).

《山东省高级人民法院关于印发基层法院民商事案件办理流程 (试行) 的通知》(鲁高法〔2019〕59号).

4.3 How to Serve Court Documents on Foreign Parties Without Domicile … 57

4.3.2 Service Under the Hague Service Convention and Other International Treaties

If the State of the person to be served has concluded a bilateral treaty with China on the service of court documents, or has acceded to the Hague Service Convention, the Chinese court will serve court documents in accordance therewith. In practice, the Hague Service Convention is also the main basis for Chinese courts to effect the service abroad.

For service abroad pursuant to the Hague Service Convention, Chinese courts usually serve court documents by forwarding to the Central Authority of the state addressed, specifically as follows:

(1) The court requesting service abroad shall submit the service request to its next higher-level court;
(2) The next higher-level court shall report the service request level by level to the SPC;
(3) The SPC will forward the service request to the Ministry of Justice; and
(4) The Ministry of Justice will send the service request to the Central Authority of the state addressed, which will then arrange the service.

It should be noted that the high courts of Beijing Municipality, Shanghai Municipality, Guangdong Province, Jiangsu Province and Zhejiang Province can directly send the service requests of their own and lower courts to the Central Authority of the state addressed, without being subject to the forwarding by the SPC and the Ministry of Justice (for details on China's court system, see Sect. 1.1).

4.3.3 Service Through Diplomatic Channels

In the absence of relevant treaties between two states, the Chinese court may, after submitting court documents to be served to the provincial high court for examination, submit them to the Department of Consular Affairs of the Ministry of Foreign Affairs, which will then forward such paperwork to the diplomatic department of the other state, which will then arrange the service.

4.3.4 Service by Mail

To the extent permitted by the internal law of the state of the person to be served, Chinese courts may serve court documents by mail. Considering the time-consuming process of cross-border mailing, under the Chinese law, in the absence of evidence of effected service (such as the service acknowledgement signed by the person to be served, the receipt record provided by the postal agency) 3 months after mailing,

Chinese courts may determine the effectiveness of the service after considering other factors (such as the submission of response documents by the person to be served). If the mail is returned with reasons indicated as "Recipient Not Found" or "Invalid Address" or other similar reasons, it shall be deemed that the service cannot be effected by mail.

4.3.5 Electronic Service

To the extent permitted by the internal law of the state of and agreed by the person to be served, Chinese courts may serve court documents on foreign parties by electronic means. For the contracting states of the Hague Service Convention that oppose service by mail, it should be presumed that they do not allow electronic service.

In addition, as reflected by the CPL Revision Draft 2022, other service methods permitted by the internal law of the state of and agreed by the person to be served is likely to be adopted by the Chinese court.

4.3.6 Service by Publication

If the service by other methods cannot be effected, the Chinese court will eventually resort to service by publication. However, the time limit of publication is 3 months, which is about 2 months longer than that of service by publication on Chinese parties. The publication may be made in newspapers of national and/or international circulation. In practice, Chinese courts will generally make publication in the overseas edition of the People's Daily (人民日报) or the China Daily (中国日报).

As reflected by the CPL Revision Draft 2022, there may be following changes to service by publication on foreign parties without domicile in China: (1) the time limit of publication is likely to be shortened to 60 days; and (2) as applied for by relevant parties, publication and other service methods can be adopted by the Chinese court simultaneously, with premises that the publication has to be made no less than 60 days in advance and service by publication will not damage the litigation rights of the party to be served.

(Reference provisions and information for Sect. 4.3).[3]

---

[3] *CPL (Revised in 2021): Article 274.*
CPL Revision Draft 2022: Article 285.
Judicial Interpretation of CPL (Revised in 2022): Article 533, 534.
Provisions of the Supreme People's Court on Service of Judicial Documents in Foreign-related Civil or Commercial Cases (Revised in 2020): Article 4.
《最高人民法院关于涉外民事或商事案件司法文书送达问题若干规定》(2020年修订).
Conference Summary 2022: Article 10–12.
Notice of the Supreme People's Court on Appointing High People's Courts of Beijing Municipality, Shanghai Municipality, Guangdong Province, Zhejiang Province and Jiangsu Province

4.4 How Do Chinese Courts Assist Foreign Courts in Service of Court Documents

4.4.1 Assistance in Service Under the Hague Service Convention

In respect of foreign court documents and related materials to be served in China under the Hague Service Convention, Chinese courts will generally provide assistance thereto according to the following procedures:

(1) The Central Authority of the requesting state submits the paperwork to the Ministry of Justice of the People's Republic of China (the Central Authority designated by the Chinese government);
(2) The Ministry of Justice forwards the paperwork to the SPC;
(3) After examining the integrity of the paperwork and confirming that there are no grounds for service refusal, the SPC forwards the paperwork to the high court of the place where the person to be served is located;
(4) The high court may either further forward the paperwork to the intermediate or primary court for service, or serve the same on its own;
(5) After the paperwork is checked as error-free and served, regardless of the effectiveness of the service, the service acknowledgement and relevant materials shall still be returned to the Ministry of Justice according to the original route; and

---

to Directly Submit and Forward Judicial Assistance Requests and Pertinent Documents to Foreign Central Authorities under the Hague Service Convention and the Hague Evidence Taking Convention (Fa Ban [2003] No.297).
《最高人民法院关于指定北京市、上海市、广东省、浙江省、江苏省高级人民法院依据海牙送达公约和海牙取证公约直接向外国中央机关提出和转递司法协助请求和相关材料的通知》(法办〔2003〕297号).
Notice of the Supreme People's Court, the Ministry of Foreign Affairs and the Ministry of Justice on the Implementation of Relevant Procedures of the Convention on the Service Abroad of Judicial and Extrajudicial Documents in Civil or Commercial Matters (Wai Fa [1992] No.8).
《最高人民法院、外交部、司法部关于执行＜关于向国外送达民事或商事司法文书和司法外文书公约＞有关程序的通知》(外发〔1992〕8号).
Notice of the Ministry of Justice, the Supreme People's Court and the Ministry of Foreign Affairs on Printing and Distributing the Implementation Measures for Implementing the Hague Service Convention (Si Fa Tong [1992] No. 093).
《司法部、最高人民法院、外交部关于印发＜关于执行海牙送达公约的实施办法＞的通知》(司发通〔1992〕093号).
Notice of the Supreme People's Court, the Ministry of Foreign Affairs and the Ministry of Justice on Several Issues Concerning Mutual Service of Court Documents Between Chinese Courts and Foreign Courts through Diplomatic Channels (Wai Fa [1986] No. 47).
《最高人民法院、外交部、司法部关于我国法院和外国法院通过外交途径相互委托送达诉讼文书若干问题的通知》(外发〔1986〕47号).

(6) The Ministry of Justice submits the paperwork to the Central Authority of the requesting state, thus completing all the procedures for assistance in service.

In the process of handling and returning the service acknowledgement, any court at any level has the power to review the materials received, so as to ensure that all the formalities comply with the Hague Service Convention and the provisions of Chinese courts. To our knowledge, it takes about four to eight months to complete all the formalities.

China, at its accession to the Hague Service Convention, made reservations to Article 10 and other provisions thereof. For example, China neither accepts service by mail from foreign courts, nor does it accept service by foreign judicial officers or parties directly through Chinese judicial officers.

4.4.2 Assistance in Service Under Bilateral Treaties

According to incomplete statistics, China has concluded 38 bilateral treaties related to the service of court documents in civil and commercial matters with France, Italy, Spain, Russia, South Korea, Singapore and other countries. These bilateral treaties also provide basis for Chinese courts to assist foreign courts in service of court documents.

If the other country is not only a contracting state to the Hague Service Convention, but also concludes a bilateral treaty with China, there will be some flexibilities for Chinese courts in the application of either the Hague Service Convention or the bilateral treaty so concluded. In handling specific matters, Chinese courts will follow the principle of reciprocity.

(Reference provisions and information for Sect. 4.4).[4]

---

[4] *Provisions of the Supreme People's Court on Judicial Assistance Requests for Service of Judicial Documents and Investigation and Evidence Collection in Handling Civil and Commercial Cases under International Conventions and Bilateral Judicial Assistance Treaties (Revised in 2020, Fa Shi [2013] No.11).*

《最高人民法院关于依据国际公约和双边司法协助条约办理民商事案件司法文书送达和调查取证司法协助请求的规定》(2020年修订, 法释〔2013〕11号).

Notice of the Supreme People's Court on Promulgation of "Implementing Rules for Provisions on Requesting Judicial Assistance in Service of Documents and Evidence Collection in Accordance with International Conventions and Bilateral Judicial Assistance Treaties (for Trial Implementation)" (Fa Fa [2013] No.6).

《最高人民法院印发 < 关于依据国际公约和双边司法协助条约办理民商事案件司法文书送达和调查取证司法协助请求的规定实施细则(试行) > 的通知》(法发[2013]6号).

Open Access This chapter is licensed under the terms of the Creative Commons Attribution 4.0 International License (http://creativecommons.org/licenses/by/4.0/), which permits use, sharing, adaptation, distribution and reproduction in any medium or format, as long as you give appropriate credit to the original author(s) and the source, provide a link to the Creative Commons license and indicate if changes were made.

The images or other third party material in this chapter are included in the chapter's Creative Commons license, unless indicated otherwise in a credit line to the material. If material is not included in the chapter's Creative Commons license and your intended use is not permitted by statutory regulation or exceeds the permitted use, you will need to obtain permission directly from the copyright holder.

Chapter 5
Trial

Abstract The pretrial preparation and trial will commence after appropriate service of the court documents on all parties. Ordinary procedure, summary procedure and special procedure are three concepts of parallel standing in the CPL. Except for cases under the summary procedure and the special procedure, all the other cases are tried under the ordinary procedure, which is the basis of all procedures and covers all necessary steps stipulated by the CPL. Our introduction will firstly be based on the ordinary procedure as well. (1) After serving court documents on all parties, the court needs to wait at least 30 days (or 45 days if the defendant is a foreign party without domicile in China) for the defendant to submit statement of defense and evidence. After that, the court can arrange a pretrial conference or a court hearing. There is no specific provision on the process and content of the pretrial conference, and in practice, the pretrial conference may proceed as an ordinary court hearing. Therefore, we advise that the parties try to figure out the process and content of the pretrial conference, and even make proper preparations with reference to the requirements of the ordinary court hearing. (2) In China, the steps of a court hearing generally include: court-conducted investigation, debates in court, closing argument and mediation. Among them, court-conducted investigation and debates in court are the core steps of court trial. To avoid unnecessary repetition and improve trial efficiency, Chinese courts sometimes combine these two steps together. During the Chinese court trial, we should pay attention to the following points: Firstly, judges are not passive listeners, but the leaders and controllers of all trial activities. Secondly, judges generally care more about the fact finding than the opinions of the parties on the law application. Thirdly, Chinese courts attach importance to the trial efficiency, and therefore the parties need to express their opinions as concisely as possible. Fourthly, the court trial may be made publicly available on the Internet; some court trials are also conducted online. (3) After finishing court hearing, the court will make the first-instance judgment and serve it on the parties through legal means to complete the rendering thereof. The parties may appeal within 15 days (or 30 days, if the appellant is a foreign party without domicile in China) and initiate the second-instance procedure. (4) Generally speaking, the trial process of second instance is not so different from that of first instance. The second-instance judgment is the effective final judgment. Under certain circumstances, the second-instance court may also remand the case to the first-instance court for retrial. (5) The trial time limit of first-instance cases under ordinary procedure is 6 months, and can be extended twice up to 15 months. The trial time limit of second-instance cases is 3 months, and can be extended once up to 6 months. But it is sometimes difficult for Chinese courts to close the case within the statutory trial time limit due to the litigation explosion. (6) In addition to the ordinary procedure, Chinese courts will try cases with little dispute and simple legal relations through the summary procedure. Cases under summary procedure are tried by one judge only, with shorter trial period and more flexible and simpler trial procedures. The summary procedure is applicable to most cases accepted by Chinese courts. However, the summary procedure is not frequently applied to foreign-related cases in China. (7) For money-judgment cases with a disputed amount below a certain standard, the trial procedure thereof will be further simplified and referred to as "Small Claims Procedure". The first instance of such cases is final, and no appeal is allowed. However, the small claims procedure is not applicable to foreign-related cases. (8) At last, all civil cases in China can be divided into two categories: foreign-related cases and non-foreign-related cases. Foreign-related cases refer to cases with foreign elements, including cases where one of the litigants is a foreigner or a foreign organization, etc. There are special rules for the trial of foreign-related cases under the Chinese legal system, mainly to protect the litigious rights of foreign parties. However, it is worth noting that if the parties submit a non-foreign-related case to a foreign court or arbitration institution, it is highly likely that Chinese courts may refuse to recognize and enforce the judgment/award so rendered. This is one of the reasons why we have to distinguish foreign-related cases from non-foreign-related cases.

5.1 Pretrial Preparations

5.1.1 Defense and Presentation of Evidence

After the case filing, the court will serve court documents on all parties. In cases under ordinary procedure, the defendant is entitled to a 15-day defense period after being served. For a foreign party without domicile in China, the defense period is 30 days.

Although the defendant fails to present his statement of defense within the defense period, he will not lose the right to defend himself in the subsequent procedure. In fact, the main function of the defense period is to determine the deadline for the defendant to raise objections to jurisdiction. If the defendant has any objection to the jurisdiction of the court accepting the case, the defendant must submit a written objection within the defense period (for objection to jurisdiction, see Sect. 2.3).

Upon expiry of the defense period and determination of the court's jurisdiction, the court will have to wait at least 15 days before arranging a pretrial conference or court hearing. This is because the time limit for presentation of evidence in cases under ordinary procedure is at least 15 days (for time limit for presentation of evidence, see Sect. 6.3).

5.1.2 Exchange of Evidence and Pretrial Conference

Chinese law stipulates that the court can prepare for the trial by organizing exchange of evidence and convening pretrial conference. Of course, if the judge deems it unnecessary, these activities may not be conducted.

The term "Exchange of Evidence" under the Chinese law mainly refers to the court organizing the parties to exchange and verify the evidence.

Comparatively speaking, the pretrial conference is more complex. The court can not only organize the exchange of evidence, but also clarify the plaintiff's claims and the defendant's defenses, deal with various applications such as obtaining evidence, and summarize the disputed issues. In practice, many judges do not strictly distinguish the exchange of evidence from the pretrial conference, and the two are often regarded as the same concept by many Chinese lawyers.

There are no specific provisions in the Chinese law on the specific process of the pretrial conference, and therefore there is much discretion vested in judges. Some judges are used to leading the whole process by asking the parties questions. Some judges hold the pretrial conference strictly in accordance with the ordinary court hearing process, and will require all parties to fully express their opinions. At this point, there is little difference between the pretrial conference and the ordinary court hearing. Therefore, if you receive a pretrial conference notice, we advise that you consult the judge about the steps and content required as much as possible. If you cannot obtain a positive reply, you'd better be well prepared for it with reference to the requirements of an ordinary court hearing.

In addition to the pretrial conference, Chinese courts often organize a trial activity called "Conversation", which is, however, not explicitly provided by the Chinese law. In practice, the steps and content of the "Conversation" vary from one case to another. The "Conversation" can be either equivalent to the exchange of evidence or the pretrial conference, or neither of the two but only a solicitation of the parties' views on specific issues (mainly the procedural arrangement of the case). Therefore, it is also of critical importance to understand the content required for the "Conversation" from the judge.

Neither the exchange of evidence nor the pretrial conference (including the "Conversation") needs to be conducted publicly, so generally, irrelevant parties are not allowed for participation therein, which is different from the formal court hearing.

(Reference provisions and information for Sect. 5.1).[1]

---

[1] *CPL (Revised in 2021): Article 128, 130, 275.*
Judicial Interpretation of CPL (Revised in 2022): Article 99, 224, 225.

5.2 Court Hearing

5.2.1 Court-Conducted Investigation

Court-conducted investigation is the first step of a court hearing. The priority of court-conducted investigation is generally to find out the basic facts of the case. If the interpretation and application of the law is the key to the case, the parties can also, as appropriate, express their opinions in this regard. Generally, court-conducted investigation will proceed as follow:

(1) The plaintiff and the defendant make their claims and defenses respectively;
(2) The plaintiff and the defendant present their evidence respectively;
(3) The plaintiff and the defendant cross examine the evidence of each other; and
(4) The judge questions either side of the case.

There are no explicit restrictions on the number and manner of questions raised by judges in the Chinese law. The judge may question either the plaintiff or the defendant or both of them. In addition, when listening to the answer of the parties, the judge may also interrupt the parties and pose another question.

After guiding the parties to express their opinions, present and cross examine evidence, the questions raised by the judge are generally highly targeted. Therefore, the parties and their lawyers need to answer the judge's questions as directly as possible and try to infer the judge's ideas from the questions.

5.2.2 Debates in Court

The term "Debates in Court" mainly refers to the parties' supplementary expression of their own views and refutation of the other party's views according to the court-conducted investigation.

According to the Chinese law, the parties can ask each other questions during debates in court. However, in practice, most judges generally do not arrange the parties to question each other. If one party requests to question the other party directly, most judges will do so personally if he/she deems the question necessary. This also reflects the fact that the judge is leading and controlling the trial procedure. Therefore, it is not common for the parties to argue with each other in China's court hearings.

In practice, the main content of both court-conducted investigation and debates in court is that the parties express their opinions to the judge and the judge asks the parties questions, without significant difference between the two. To avoid unnecessary repetition and improve trial efficiency, Chinese law stipulates that judges can combine court-conducted investigation and debates in court together with the consent of the parties.

5.2.3 Closing Argument

At the end of debates in court, the parties still have the right to make a closing argument. However, under most circumstances, the judge only wants the parties to confirm their claims and previous opinions at this point.

Therefore, we strongly advise that the parties express all their opinions in court-conducted investigation and debates in court, rather than deliberately withholding them until the closing argument. If additional comments are indeed necessary, they should be presented as concise as possible.

5.2.4 Mediation

Before the end of the trial, the judge will generally try to organize the parties for mediation. If the court-connected mediation fails, the judge may also organize the parties for out-of-court mediation after the court hearing. In addition, some judges will also try to organize the parties for mediation before the trial (for mediation and settlement, see Chap. 11).

5.2.5 Noteworthy Points in Court Hearing

5.2.5.1 The Court Hearing is Fully Dominated by the Judge

China adopts the inquisitorial system for its court trial. Judges are not passive listeners, but the leaders and controllers of all trial activities. All trial activities should be carried out under the auspices of the judges. During the court hearing, the parties must obey the instructions of the judges, and obtain the consent of the judges before expressing opinions and taking other actions.

Most of the time, the parties should express their opinions to the judges rather than the other party; direct argument and cross-examination between the parties are not common in China's court hearing. Therefore, the parties need to focus on expressing their opinions to and answering the questions of the judges, rather than argument and cross-examination with the other party.

5.2.5.2 The Priority of Court Hearing is to Find Out the Facts

Finding out the facts of the case and accurately applying the law are two prerequisites for making a judgment. In China, judges can study the interpretation and application of law after court hearing, but the fact-finding must rely on the statements and evidence presentation of the parties during the court hearing. Therefore, during the court hearing, Chinese judges tend to focus more on finding out the facts rather than listening to the opinions of the parties on the law application.

5.2.5.3 The Opinions Should Be Expressed as Concisely as Possible Due to Limited Court Hearing Time

Restrained by manpower, in China, judges will generally limit the trial time as far as possible. Under most circumstances, one court hearing session will not last more than half a day.

For the number of court hearing sessions, there is no explicit limit for cases under ordinary procedure. In practice, given that there are legal restrictions on the trial period, and besides, the pretrial conference and the "Conversation" mentioned previously can also partially achieve the purpose of court trial, most judges will try to control the number of trial sessions.

Due to the limit of trial time, most Chinese judges attach great importance to the trial efficiency, and resent long speeches and repetitive opinions of the parties. Therefore, the opinions of the parties should be as concise as possible, and the answers to the judges' questions should be as brief and direct as possible.

5.2.5.4 The Court Hearing Can Be Streamed Live on the Internet or Even Conducted Through the Internet

The court hearing of most cases needs to be conducted in an open court (except for divorce cases, cases involving trade secrets, etc.), and the public can apply to the court for on-site attendance at the court hearing. In addition, the Chinese court will also make some court hearings available live online through China Court Trial Online (http://tingshen.court.gov.cn/), which would attract tens of millions of viewers in terms of high-profile cases. Therefore, if you do not want the case to be heard in an open court, you'd better take the initiative to apply to the court for a private hearing with legal grounds.

Beijing Internet Court, Hangzhou Internet Court and Guangzhou Internet Court try their cases almost all through the Internet. Due to the Covid-19, other Chinese courts have also set their feet in online trial. Some courts have developed special online trial software, while others conduct online court hearing with the help of third-party online video conferencing software. However, the consent of the parties is required for the court hearing to be conducted through the Internet.

(Reference provisions and information for Sect. 5.2).[2]

---

[2] *CPL (Revised in 2021): Article 16, 137, 141, 144, 145.*
 Judicial Interpretation of CPL (Revised in 2022): Article 228, 230.
 Online Litigation Rules for People's Courts (Fa Shi [2021] No.12).
 《人民法院在线诉讼规则》(法释〔2021〕12号).

5.3 First-Instance Judgment

Theoretically, the court can make a judgment immediately after the end of the court hearing. However, in practice, it still takes a while before the parties can receive a judgment. The court, after making the judgment, needs to serve the same on the parties to complete the rendering thereof. The court may serve the judgment on the parties by special mail, or by notifying the parties to personally come to the court to receive the judgment. The court may also serve the judgment on the parties by other methods for service of court documents (for service of court documents, see Chap. 4).

The judgment, in addition to being served on the parties, should also be posted on China Judgments Online (https://wenshu.court.gov.cn/), unless state secrets, juvenile delinquency, divorce and other special circumstances are involved. Before posting the judgment, the court shall process the personal information of the parties as appropriate to protect their personal privacy. Notwithstanding the foregoing provisions, a considerable number of judgments have not been posted online in practice. We do hope this will change to the better in the future.

If neither of the parties has appealed, the first-instance judgment shall enter into force, and the winning party can apply to the court for enforcement (for enforcement, see Chap. 10).

(Reference provisions and information for Sect. 5.3).[3]

5.4 Second-Instance Procedure

If either party is dissatisfied with the first-instance judgment, it may submit a written appeal to initiate the second-instance procedure within 15 days upon receipt of the first-instance judgment. For a foreign party without domicile in Mainland China, the time limit for submitting a written appeal will be extended to 30 days upon receipt of the first-instance judgment.

A second-instance case shall also be tried by a collegial panel composed of three or more judges. However, for some simple cases, if agreed by both parties, they can be heard by one judge. Unlike first-instance cases, there will be no people's assessor in the collegial panel of second-instance cases.

Generally speaking, the trial process of second instance is not so different from that of first instance. However, if the parties do not present new facts, evidence and reasons, and the court believes that it is not necessary to hold a formal court hearing for some reasons (for example, the facts found in the first instance are clear and

---

[3] *CPL (Revised in 2021): Article 41.*

Provisions of the Supreme People's Court on Publishing Judgment Documents on the Internet by People's Courts (Revised in 2016, Fa Shi [2016] No.19).

《最高人民法院关于人民法院在互联网公布裁判文书的规定》 (2016修订, 法释〔2016〕19号)

there is only error in the application of law), the court may make a judgment without holding a court hearing. In practice, the second-instance court often appoints an undertaking judge to have a conversation with the parties to fully understand the case and listen to the opinions of the parties, and then decides on the necessity of a formal court hearing. Therefore, even if there is no formal court hearing in the second instance, the parties would generally still have the opportunity to make statements and express their opinions to the judge.

After the second-instance judgment is made and served on the parties, the winning party can apply to the court for enforcement. If the second-instance court considers that the first-instance court has not tried the basic facts, or there are material violations of due process such as the omission of a party to the case, it may also reverse the first-instance judgment and remand it to the first-instance court for retrial.

If either party is dissatisfied with the second-instance judgment, the party concerned may apply to a higher court for retrial, or even request the procuratorate to re-examine the case. However, in practice, it is quite difficult to initiate the retrial or the procuratorate reexamination (for application for retrial and procuratorate reexamination, see Sect. 1.2).

(Reference provisions and information for Sect. 5.4).[4]

5.5 Time Limit for Trial

The trial time limit commences from the case filing until the case closed. The term "case closed" may refer to either the judge making a judgment on the case, or the parties reaching a settlement agreement, or the plaintiff withdrawing the action. However, the time for the service of court documents, resolving disputes over jurisdiction, conducting examination or appraisal, negotiation and settlement shall be excluded from the trial time limit.

The trial time limit of first-instance cases under ordinary procedure is 6 months, and can be extended twice up to 15 months. The trial time limit of second-instance cases is 3 months, and can be extended once up to 6 months.

In practice, Chinese courts will regularly assess the number and proportion of cases not closed of each judge, which is of important reference value in determining the promotion and benefits of judges. Therefore, most Chinese judges will adopt various methods, including mediation, to close the case as soon as possible. However, due to the litigation explosion (especially in economically developed areas), it is sometimes difficult for Chinese courts to close the case within the statutory trial time limit. Therefore, we hope that the reform of separating cases into ordinary procedure and

---

[4] *CPL (Revised in 2021): Article 151, 171, 176, 177, 181, 182, 276.*

Provisions of the Supreme People's Court on Several Issues Relating to Ordering Retrial and Remand in Civil Trial Supervisory Procedures (Fa Shi [2015] No.7).

《最高人民法院关于民事审判监督程序严格依法适用指令再审和发回重审若干问题的规定》(法释〔2015〕7号).

summary procedure respectively can help Chinese courts continuously improve trial efficiency.

It should be noted that foreign-related cases (see Sect. 5.8) are not subject to the trial time limit. However, constrained by the court's performance assessment system, judges will never postpone the trial to an indefinite period.

(Reference provisions and information for Sect. 5.5).[5]

5.6 Summary Procedure

5.6.1 What Is Summary Procedure?

Summary procedure is a concept in parallel standing with the ordinary procedure. Chinese law stipulates that the summary procedure is applicable to simple civil cases with clear-cut facts, rights and obligations and easy-to-resolve dispute tried by primary courts and dispatched tribunals thereof.

However, Chinese law, though enumerates the types of cases that cannot be tried through summary procedure (such as cases in which the whereabouts of the defendant is unknown at the time of action, cases in which the parties on one side are numerous, cases involving national interests or public interests, etc.), fails to provide more detailed guidance on the application standard of summary procedure. In practice, each court has its discretion to decide the application scope of summary procedure.

In addition to the court's decision to apply the summary procedure, the parties may also take the initiative to agree on the application of summary procedure before the court hearing. However, in practice, this situation is rarely seen. If the parties do not agree to apply the summary procedure, they may raise an objection to the court, which shall then decide whether to apply the ordinary procedure instead. If the court finds that it'd be better not to apply the summary procedure during the trial, it may also apply the ordinary procedure ex officio.

According to the Work Report of the SPC issued in March 2018, 47.835 million civil and commercial cases were closed by Chinese courts from 2013 to 2017, of which 32.416 million cases were closed under the summary procedure (including the small claims procedure), accounting for more than two-thirds of all closed cases. This efficient and convenient trial procedure plays an important role in China's judicial system.

However, for foreign-related civil cases, Chinese courts do not frequently apply the summary procedure.

---

[5] *CPL (Revised in 2021): Article 152, 183, 277.*

Provisions of the Supreme People's Court on the Strict Implementation of the Time Limit System for Case Trial (Revised in 2008, Fa Shi [2000] No.29): Article 2.

《最高人民法院关于严格执行案件审理期限制度的若干规定》(2008年修订，法释〔2000〕29号).

5.6.2 Difference Between Summary Procedure and Ordinary Procedure

5.6.2.1 Only One Judge for Case Trial

Cases under formal procedure shall be tried by a collegial panel composed of three or more judges (and people's assessors, if any), unless specific conditions for one-judge trial are met. However, all cases under summary procedure are heard by only one judge.

5.6.2.2 Simpler and More Flexible Trial Procedure

In cases under ordinary procedure, the defendant's defense period after being served is fixed at 15 days, and the time limit for evidence presentation specified by the court shall not be less than 15 days. Before the court hearing, the court shall notify the parties at least 3 days in advance. Besides, there is also no explicit limit on the number of trial sessions.

However, in cases under summary procedure, the court may shorten the defendant's defense period, and the time limit for evidence presentation specified by the court shall not exceed 15 days. The court may notify the parties orally of the hearing at any time. In principle, there will be only one trial session.

The above is a non-exhaustive enumeration of the differences between the two. In short, the trial of cases under summary procedure is simpler and more flexible.

5.6.2.3 Shorter Trial Period

The trial period of cases under ordinary procedure is 6 months, and can be extended twice up to 15 months; the trial period of cases under summary procedure is 3 months, and can only be extended once up to 4 months. However, foreign-related cases (whether under ordinary procedure or summary procedure) are not subject to the above-mentioned time limit.

5.6.2.4 Lower Court Costs

For cases under summary procedure, Chinese courts charge the court costs at 50% of that of cases under ordinary procedure (for court costs, see Sect. 1.5). Obviously, the application of summary procedure can effectively reduce the litigation costs.

(Reference provisions and information for Sect. 5.6).[6]

---

[6] *CPL (Revised in 2021): Article 160, 163, 164, 170.*
Judicial Interpretation of CPL (Revised in 2022): Article 257, 261, 266, 267.

5.7 Small Claims Procedure—A Further Simplified Summary Procedure

Among cases under summary procedure, if the case is a pure money-judgment one with a disputed amount less than 50% of the average annual salary of the previous year (hereinafter referred to as the "Average Social Salary") in the provincial administrative region where the court is located, the small claims procedure shall be applied. Even if the disputed amount ranges from 50 to 200% of the Average Social Salary, the parties may also apply the small claims procedure by agreement.

The most prominent feature of small claims procedure is that the first-instance judgment takes effect immediately without being subject to appeal by the parties (for China's hierarchical trial system, see Sect. 1.2). Once the judgment is made, the wining party may apply for enforcement in accordance with the judgment.

Generally, the defense period of small claims cases shall not exceed 7 days, and the period of evidence presentation shall not exceed 15 days.

In terms of the trial period, it is only 2 months for small claims cases, or up to 3 months after one extension.

In addition, the court can simplify the judgment of small claims cases. In practice, some courts use standard forms to prepare the judgment of small claims cases.

Chinese law also enumerates cases that should not be subject to small claims procedure. However, it should be noted that small claims procedure is not applicable to foreign-related cases regardless of their disputed amount.

(Reference provisions and information for Sect. 5.7).[7]

Provisions of the Supreme People's Court on Applying Summary Procedure in Trial of Civil Cases (Revised in 2020, Fa Shi [2003] No.5): Article 23.
《最高人民法院关于适用简易程序审理民事案件的若干规定》(2020年修订，法释〔2003〕15号).
Measures for the Payment of Litigation Fees: Article 16.
《诉讼费用交纳办法》.

[7] *CPL (Revised in 2021): Article 165, 166, 168.*
Judicial Interpretation of CPL (Revised in 2022): Article 275, 280.
Provisions of the Supreme People's Court on Applying Summary Procedure in Trial of Civil Cases (Revised in 2020, Fa Shi [2003] No.5): Article 23.
《最高人民法院关于适用简易程序审理民事案件的若干规定》(2020年修订，法释〔2003〕15号).
Measures for the Payment of Litigation Fees: Article 16.
《诉讼费用交纳办法》.

5.8 Foreign-Related Cases—Special Rules for Foreign Parties' Participation in China's Litigation

5.8.1 What Are Foreign-Related Cases?

A case is a foreign-related one under the Chinese law if it satisfies any of the following conditions:

(1) One of the litigants is a foreigner or a foreign organization;
(2) One of the litigants has his/her habitual residence outside China;
(3) The subject matter of the case is outside China; or
(4) The facts that establish, change, or terminate the civil-law relations occur outside China;

The term "foreign organization" mentioned herein refers to an organization registered outside China. Foreign-invested enterprises, including Joint Venture (JV) and Wholly Foreign Owned Enterprise (WFOE), established in China by foreign parties are registered in China and therefore cannot be regarded as foreign organizations.

In practice, very few cases, though do not satisfy the above conditions, are still regarded as foreign-related cases because of other "foreign elements".

Given that Hong Kong S.A.R., Macau S.A.R., Taiwan region and the Mainland China are of different jurisdictions, cases involving Hong Kong S.A.R., Macau S.A.R., and Taiwan region shall be, mutatis mutandis, subject to the provisions on foreign-related cases.

5.8.2 What Is Special About Foreign-Related Cases?

Compared with non-foreign-related cases, the procedures and substantive issues of foreign-related cases are often more complicated. Therefore, Part Four of the CPL and relevant judicial interpretations have made several special rules for foreign-related cases. Among them, those rules of more frequent application include:

Firstly, identity documents and authorization documents submitted by foreign parties to the court are generally required to be notarized and authenticated (for materials required to be submitted for participation in China's litigation, see Sect. 3.1).

Secondly, jurisdiction of the case. Chinese courts may have jurisdiction over the case even if the connecting factor under the general rules on jurisdiction does not relate to the Chinese mainland (for connecting factors of special jurisdiction of foreign-related cases, see Sect. 2.2.9). For some special types of cases, the parties cannot be subject to the jurisdiction of foreign courts by agreement, except for agreement on arbitration (for exclusive jurisdiction, see Sect. 2.2.7).

Thirdly, the rules for service of court documents on foreign parties are more rigorous and complicated. If court documents are served by publication, the publication period is 3 months, 2 months longer than that within China (for service on foreign parties, see Sect. 4.3).

Fourthly, the defense period and appeal period for foreign parties are generally 30 days, 15 days longer than that for Chinese parties (for defense period, see Sect. 5.1.1; for appeal period, see Sect. 5.4).

Fifthly, foreign-related cases are not subject to the trial time limit (for trial time limit, see Sect. 5.5).

Sixthly, foreign-related cases are neither subject to the small claims procedure where the first instance is final, nor subject to the summary procedure under most circumstances (for summary procedure and small claims procedure, see Sects. 5.6 and 5.7).

Due to the complexity of foreign-related cases (especially foreign-related commercial cases), Chinese courts are promoting the centralized trial of foreign-related commercial cases. In other words, foreign-related commercial cases will be subject to the jurisdiction of specific courts (such as the Beijing Fourth Intermediate People's Court), specific trial divisions or even specific judges of a court. This practice is helpful to improve the trial quality.

5.8.3 Prohibition on Submitting Non-Foreign-Related Cases to Foreign Courts or Arbitration Institutions

If the parties submit a non-foreign-related case to a foreign court or arbitration institution, it is highly likely that Chinese courts may refuse to recognize and enforce the judgment or award so rendered.

For example, in a dispute arising from the transfer of a golf course in Beijing, one party submitted the dispute to the Korean Commercial Arbitration Board (KCAB) for arbitration according to the arbitration agreement and won the case, and then applied for recognition and enforcement of the arbitral award in Beijing. However, the SPC held that, given the Chinese law did not authorize the parties to submit non-foreign-related disputes to foreign arbitration institutions or ad hoc arbitration outside China, the SPC found the arbitration agreement invalid, and refused to recognize and enforce the arbitral award so rendered.

However, it should be noted that, if a WFOE established in a pilot free trade zone submits any dispute to a foreign arbitration institution, Chinese courts tend to adopt a more relaxed attitude under such circumstance.

For example, in a dispute arising from equipment purchase in Shanghai between two WFOEs established in the Shanghai Pilot Free Trade Zone, one party submitted the dispute to the Singapore International Arbitration Centre (SIAC) for arbitration and won the case, and then applied for recognition and enforcement of the arbitral award in Shanghai. The other party raised an objection on the grounds that the dispute was not a foreign-related one and the arbitration agreement was invalid. However, the SPC found the dispute as a foreign-related one and further recognized and enforced the arbitral award for the following reasons: both WFOEs were registered in the Shanghai Pilot Free Trade Zone, having close connections with their foreign investors; moreover, the equipment in this case was bonded goods, which could not be delivered to the buyer before customs clearance; therefore, the equipment purchase contract was somehow related to the international sale of goods. Later, the SPC issued a document to relax the review standards for foreign-related cases relating to free trade zones.

With China's further opening up to the outside world, we believe that Chinese courts will apply more flexible standards to determine foreign-related cases, and will also handle foreign-related cases with a more open and friendly attitude.

(Reference provisions and information for Sect. 5.8).[8]

Open Access This chapter is licensed under the terms of the Creative Commons Attribution 4.0 International License (http://creativecommons.org/licenses/by/4.0/), which permits use, sharing, adaptation, distribution and reproduction in any medium or format, as long as you give appropriate credit to the original author(s) and the source, provide a link to the Creative Commons license and indicate if changes were made.

The images or other third party material in this chapter are included in the chapter's Creative Commons license, unless indicated otherwise in a credit line to the material. If material is not included in the chapter's Creative Commons license and your intended use is not permitted by statutory regulation or exceeds the permitted use, you will need to obtain permission directly from the copyright holder.

---

[8] *CPL (Revised in 2021): Article 271–277.*

Judicial Interpretation of CPL (Revised in 2022): Article 520, 521, 525.

Provisions of the Supreme People's Court on Several Issues Concerning Jurisdiction over Foreign-Related Civil and Commercial Cases (Fa Shi [2022] No.18): Article 4, 5.

《最高人民法院关于涉外民商事案件管辖若干问题的规定》(法释〔2022〕18号).

Reply of the Supreme People's Court on the Application of Beijing Chaolai Xinsheng Sports and Leisure Co., Ltd. (北京朝来新生体育休闲有限公司) for Recognition of Arbitral Awards No. 12113–0011 and No. 12112–0012 Rendered by the Korean Commercial Arbitration Board ([2013] Min Si Ta Zi No. 64).

《最高人民法院关于北京朝来新生体育休闲有限公司申请承认大韩商事仲裁院作出的第12113-0011号、第12112-0012号仲裁裁决案件请示的复函》(〔2013〕民四他字第64号).

Reply of the Supreme People's Court on the Application of Siemens International Trade (Shanghai) Co., Ltd. (西门子国际贸易 (上海) 有限公司) for Recognition and Enforcement of Foreign Arbitral Award ([2015] Min Si Ta Zi No. 5).

《最高人民法院关于西门子国际贸易 (上海) 有限公司申请承认与执行外国仲裁裁决一案的请示的复函》(〔2013〕民四他字第5号).

Opinions of the Supreme People's Court on Providing Judicial Guarantee for the Development of Free Trade Zones (Fa Fa [2016] No.34): Article 9.

《最高人民法院关于为自由贸易试验区建设提供司法保障的意见》(法发〔2016〕34号).

Chapter 6
Evidence

Abstract Evidence is a topic we would like to spend a large number of pages to introduce. China's civil litigation evidence system is featured by highly distinctive characteristics from basic concepts to specific rules. For example, the Chinese law emphasizes the principle of "the burden of proof lies with the party asserting a proposition"; the parties should collect evidence on their own as far as possible, rather than relying on the other party to provide evidence. For another example, compared with the witness testimony, the Chinese law attaches more importance to the documentary evidence. On the basis of these characteristics, we strive to comb through and introduce China's civil litigation evidence system as comprehensively as possible. First, we will introduce some basic systems, including standard of proof, burden of proof, time limit for presenting evidence, and self-admission system. Second, we will introduce some specific types of evidence that readers may be interested in, including witness testimony, secret recording, and evidence from the Internet and social media. Under the Chinese law, the admissibility, probative force, evidence collection and application methods of such evidence all have their own distinctive characteristics, and therefore will be introduced in more detail. Third, we will introduce, in addition to presentation of evidence by the parties, other evidence systems, including technical examination officer, expert opinions/appraisal and examination, evidence investigation and collection by the court, evidence preservation by the court, and evidence presentation order. The parties may, when encountering difficulties in presenting evidence on their own, consider using these systems to obtain evidence or shift the burden of proof. At last, how to keep evidence confidential in litigation is also a highly practical question frequently asked by our peers. We would like to share our thoughts on this issue in the last section of this chapter.

6.1 Standard of Proof

Standard of proof refers to the degree of evidence necessary to establish proof in a court proceeding. The standards of proof in China's civil litigation can be categorized into two groups: most to-be-proved facts are subject to the standard of "preponderance of the evidence"(高度可能性), and some special to-be-proved facts subject to the standard of "beyond a reasonable doubt" (排除合理怀疑).

6.1.1 Most To-Be-Proved Facts Subject to "Preponderance of the Evidence" Standard

As the name implies, "preponderance" refers to the fact that the existing evidence has shown that the fact to be proven is more probable than not. "Preponderance" does not require the evidence to reach the extent of beyond a reasonable doubt, and some judges describe it as reaching the possibility of 75%.

Given the different circumstances in each case, as well as the different personal experience and knowledge of each judge, the Chinese law does not specifically provide for "preponderance", but gives the judge the discretion to make judgment therefor. In practice, some judges think that "preponderance" can be further divided into three levels: highest possibility, higher possibility and high possibility. It can be seen that "preponderance" is a rather flexible standard, and judges need to determine whether the evidence meets the standard of proof based on the law and their personal experience.

6.1.2 Special To-Be-Proved Facts Subject to "Beyond a Reasonable Doubt" Standard

Some special facts to be proved need to meet the standard of "beyond a reasonable doubt" only applicable in criminal cases. "Beyond a reasonable doubt", obviously more demanding than "preponderance", mainly applies to the following to-be-proved facts.

Firstly, fraud, coercion and malicious collusion. Fraud, coercion and malicious collusion are the statutory reasons for the parties to claim rescission or invalidation of the contract. Chinese laws increase the standards of proof for these matters for two reasons: the subjective psychological state needs to be proved by sufficient evidence; to avoid the contract effectiveness being easily shaken and to enhance the stability and security of the transaction as much as possible.

Secondly, oral will. An oral will is made by the testator orally in a critical situation. Once there is a lawsuit about the authenticity of an oral will, it often involves many unknown related problems, such as the mental state of the testator, the integrity of the witness and whether the witness has a stake in the heir. Therefore, the statutory standard of proof is relatively high.

Thirdly, gift. Gift (especially the gift with high value) may involve complex reasons, such as repayment of gambling debt, gift due to extramarital affairs, or other conditional gifts. Raising the standard of proof can avoid neglecting the hidden doubts and reduce the possibility of misjudgment.

(Reference provisions and information for Sect. 6.1).[1]

6.2 Burden of Proof

"The burden of proof lies with the party asserting a proposition" is a primary rule of burden of proof in China's judicial proceedings. Only under exceptional circumstances can the parties request the court to assist in obtaining evidence or the other party to present evidence. The burden of proof is not unchangeable, which can shift from one party to the other during the trial. The judge has some discretion on the distribution of the burden of proof.

In respect of some special cases or special facts to be proved, Chinese law reverses the burden of proof to be borne by the opposing party, instead of the party which makes such claim or statement.

6.2.1 What Is Burden of Proof

If a fact to be proved is found untenable by the court on the grounds of insufficient evidence, such an adverse consequence is called burden of proof. Therefore, the distribution rule of the burden of proof is to determine which party should prove the fact in dispute.

6.2.2 Core of the Rule—The Burden of Proof Lies with the Party Asserting a Proposition

"The burden of proof lies with the party asserting a proposition" is the core of the burden of proof. For example, in a tort case where the plaintiff claims that the defendant's act constitutes an infringement, while the defendant claims that there are reasons for liability exemption/reduction, the plaintiff needs to present evidence on tort, damage consequence, causality, and the defendant's fault, while the defendant needs to present evidence on the existence of the reason for liability exemption/reduction.

Based on this rule, the first obligor of evidence presentation is always the parties themselves, and the parties should try their best to obtain the evidence. Only when the parties are unable to obtain evidence for objective reasons, can they request the court to assist in the investigation and collection of evidence, take evidence preservation

---

[1] *Judicial Interpretation of CPL (Revised in 2022): Article 108, 109.*

measures, or order the other party to present evidence (for court's investigation and collection of evidence, see Sect. 6.11; for evidence preservation, see Sect. 6.13; for evidence presentation order, see Sect. 6.14).

In addition, "the burden of proof lies with the party asserting a proposition" means that the parties generally only need to present evidence for the facts they claim, rather than all the facts involved in the case. Meanwhile, the parties may select evidence for presentation at their discretion. Choosing appropriate evidence is the key to winning a case, and the parties often need experienced lawyers in formulating strategies therefor.

6.2.3 The Shift in the Burden of Proof

After the party asserting the affirmative assumes the burden of proof, if the judge thinks that the evidence is sufficient, then the burden of proof will shift to the opposing party. In other words, the respondent shall present rebuttal evidence to sway the judge's inner judgment, otherwise, it shall bear the adverse consequences. Therefore, whether the burden of proof is transferred or not depends entirely on the judge. However, the judge generally will not disclose his/her judgment, which may have changed a few times as the court proceedings go. Therefore, the transfer of the burden of proof is often not obvious. The parties can only tell from the judge's questions. Needless to say, hiring experienced lawyers is very necessary.

6.2.4 The Reversal of the Burden of Proof

In some cases, there is a big gap between the two sides in terms of legal knowledge and the ability of evidence presentation, and therefore the law needs to favor the weaker side. In addition, for some special facts to be proved, it is often difficult for the claimant to present evidence. Under such circumstances, the regular rule of presenting evidence is no longer applicable, and the burden of proof will be borne by the opposing party. The common cases of reversal of the burden of proof in practice are as follows:

(1) In the case of employment dispute arising from the employer's decision to rescind the employment contract, reduce the remuneration, and calculate the employee's seniority, it should be the employer proving the lawfulness of its behavior, rather than the employee proving the unlawfulness of the employer's behavior;
(2) In the case of patent infringement of the new product manufacturing method, it should be the alleged infringer proving the difference, rather than the patentee proving the consistency between the product manufacturing methods;

(3) In the case of personal injury caused by objects falling from buildings, structures or other facilities, it should be the owner, the manager or the user of the above-mentioned objects proving their innocence, rather than the injured party proving the fault of such persons; and
(4) In the case of environmental pollution, it should be the polluter proving the non-existence of causality between his behavior and environmental damage, rather than the injured party proving the causality thereof.

In addition, when the evidence is controlled by the other party, the party asserting the affirmative may apply to the court to require the other party to disclose the relevant evidence (for evidence presentation order, see Sect. 6.14). From the jurisprudence perspective, it is still controversial to categorize this rule as the reversal of the burden of proof; however, we believe that it does produce the effect that the reversal of the burden of proof possesses.

After the party presents certain evidence as required by the rules of reversal of burden of proof, the burden of proof may also shift to the other party as introduced before.

(Reference provisions and information for Sect. 6.2).[2]

6.3 Time Limit for Presenting Evidence

To participate in China's judicial proceedings, it is important to understand the time limit system for presenting evidence. The time limit for presenting evidence is generally designated by the court and may be changed under some circumstances. Although the evidence is still very much likely to be admitted by the court even if its presentation is delayed and may incur court punishment, the parties should try the best to present evidence on time.

Some parties may adopt the strategy of a surprise attack, that is, to present evidence without prior disclosure during the court trial. For general evidence, the parties may conduct a preliminary examination on the spot and make it clear to the judge that they reserve the right to supplement and modify the examination opinions in the future. For critical or complex evidence, we advise our clients not to conduct an examination on the spot, but to apply to the court for extra time for evidence examination.

---

[2] *CPL (Revised in 2021): Article 64.*
Judicial Interpretation of CPL (Revised in 2022): Article 90, 91.
Civil Code of the People's Republic of China (Promulgated in 2020): Article 1230, 1253.
《中华人民共和国民法典》(2020年公布).
Patent Law of the People's Republic of China (Revised in 2020): Article 66.
《中华人民共和国专利法》(2020年修订).
Interpretation of the Supreme People's Court on Issues Concerning the Application of Law in the Trial of Labor Dispute Cases (I) (Fa Shi [2020] No.26): Article 44.
《最高人民法院关于审理劳动争议案件适用法律问题的解释 (一)》(法释〔2020〕26号).

6.3.1 What Is Time Limit for Presenting Evidence

As the name suggests, time limit for presenting evidence is the time limit for the parties to present evidence to the court. In addition, the applications to the court for evidence investigation and collection, evidence preservation, examination and appraisal and the like also need to be submitted before the expiration of the time limit for presenting evidence.

6.3.2 How to Determine the Time Limit for Presenting Evidence

The time limit for presenting evidence is generally designated by the court, or sometimes agreed upon by the parties. However, in practice, it is designated by the court in most cases, and the latter situation is very rare.

The time limit for presenting evidence designated by the court commences from the expiration of the defense period, and shall meet the following requirements:

(1) No less than 15 days in the first-instance trial in which the ordinary procedure is applied;
(2) No more than 15 days in the first-instance trial in which the summary procedure is applied; and
(3) No less than 10 days in the second-instance trial in which the parties present new evidence.

The time limit for presenting evidence is not unchangeable. If the parties have justified reasons, they may apply to the court for an extension of time before the period expires. After the expiration of the time limit for presenting evidence, if one party needs to present rebuttal evidence against the other party, or needs to supplement/correct the source/form of their own evidence, it can also apply to the court to re-determine the time limit for presenting evidence.

In practice, some judges will not define the time limit for presenting evidence before the trial, but will, during the trial, determine a certain number of days after the trial as the time limit for presenting evidence.

6.3.3 Legal Consequences of Late Evidence Presentation

Before the revision of the CPL in 2012, Chinese courts had strict requirements on the time limit for presenting evidence and would not accept late evidence presentation in principle. The revised CPL has relaxed the requirement on such limit. If the parties present evidence late, according to the merits of cases and the parties' subjective fault, the court may choose to not to admit the late presented evidence, or to admit the evidence after admonishing and imposing fines (less than CNY 100,000 for natural persons; CNY 50,000–CNY 1,000,000 for organizations) on the parties.

Viewed from the judicial practice, China's judicial system attaches great importance to fact-finding. As long as the late presented evidence contributes to the fact-finding, judges generally tend to admit such evidence. Nevertheless, we would still advise our clients to present evidence as scheduled to avoid the above adverse consequences.

6.3.4 How to Deal with Surprise Evidence

Because some judges do not strictly define the time limit for presenting evidence, some parties may adopt the strategy of a surprise attack, that is, to present evidence without prior disclosure during the court trial. Even if the judge designates the time limit for presenting evidence as before the court session, due to the lack of severe consequences of late presentation, some parties may still choose to use surprise evidence. Under such circumstances, it is often difficult for the opposing party to give effective examination opinions to challenge the evidence on the spot, while it may leave a negative impression on the judge if the party concerned completely refuses to do so.

In the face of surprise evidence, we'd give the following advice:

Firstly, for general evidence, the parties may conduct a preliminary examination on the spot and make it clear to the judge that they reserve the right to supplement and modify the examination opinions in the future. If the party finds significant defects of the other party's evidence on the spot, it shall point them out immediately to win the favor of the judge to the greatest extent.

Secondly, for critical or complex evidence, we advise our clients not to conduct an examination on the spot, but to apply to the court for extra time for evidence examination. According to our experience, the first-time examination opinions would have a great influence on judges. A reckless examination would probably lead to the judge's negative impression on us, which is difficult to be reversed even if formal opinions are submitted later.

Thirdly, according to Chinese laws, if one party fails to raise an objection to the other party's late evidence presentation, such late evidence presentation will not be deemed as late. Therefore, the parties may raise objections to the surprise evidence and request the judge to consider admonition and fine to the other party.

It should be noted that we do not recommend our clients to present surprise evidence without careful consideration. Not only is it not conducive to the judge's in-depth understanding of our evidence before the trial, but also will it cause an additional burden for the judge to preside over the trial, and even cause the judge's antipathy. It will not be worth the candle to intentionally use the surprise evidence but to have the consequence of non-admission, or even admonishment and fine by the judge. Therefore, it is necessary for the parties to provide reasonable explanations and apologies to the judges in the case of late evidence presentation either due to obtaining the evidence late or intentionally making an evidence surprise attack at some times.

(Reference provisions and information for Sect. 6.3).[3]

6.4 Self-admission System

The self-admission system in the civil procedure means that, during the litigation, once one party states or explicitly acknowledges the facts against itself, the other party can be exempt from the burden of proof for these facts. The self-admission is the disposition of the litigant's procedural rights, and may have a substantive impact on the fact-finding and the burden of proof. It is very important for the litigants to understand the elements of self-admission, in order to avoid wrongly-made self-admission and take advantage of the self-admission made by the other party.

As to some special circumstances related to self-admission, such as self-admission made in another case, acknowledgement made in mediation and settlement, etc., this section introduces as follows based on law and judicial practice in China.

6.4.1 What Adverse Statement Would Constitute Self-admission?

According to Chinese law, a party's statement or explicit acknowledgment of the facts against itself during the litigation constitutes self-admission. In this regard, we'd like to specify the following points:

Firstly, self-admission needs to be made during the litigation, not only including oral confession made in a court trial, pre-trial meeting, etc., but also confession made in the documents submitted to the court and the other party.

Secondly, self-admission can only aim at the facts of the case, but not the legal issues.

Thirdly, self-admission includes both the voluntary statement of one party and the acknowledgment of the other party's statement. If one party neither confirms nor denies the fact against it proposed by the other party, and still refuses to express its confirmation or denial upon explanation by the judges, it shall be deemed as acknowledging the fact so proposed.

---

[3] *CPL (Revised in 2021): Article 7, 68, 118, 142.*
Judicial Interpretation of CPL (Revised in 2022): Article 99–102.
Provisions of the Supreme People's Court on Applying Summary Procedure in Trial of Civil Cases (Revised in 2020, Fa Shi [2003] No.5): Article 22.
《最高人民法院关于适用简易程序审理民事案件的若干规定》(2020年修订，法释〔2003〕15号).
Judicial Interpretation on Civil Evidence (Revised in 2019): Article 51, 59.

Fourthly, the self-admission of the attorney within the authorization shall also be deemed as the self-admission of the party itself, unless the party concerned denies it on the spot.

Fifthly, the self-admission rule does not apply to the facts involving personal status, national interests and social/public interests.

6.4.2 The Legal Effect of Self-admission

For the adverse facts admitted by one party, the other party no longer needs to bear the burden of proof, and the court may directly determine the facts of the case based on the self-admission.

In principle, the self-admission is irrevocable once made, unless the other party agrees so, or the self-admission is made under duress or based on major misunderstanding. In the absence of the above circumstances, if the parties want to revoke the self-admitted facts, they must provide sufficient evidence to prove the contrary, otherwise the court can still make a decision based on the self-admitted facts.

It should be noted that the court has the right not to admit the self-admitted fact if it is inconsistent with the fact proved by other evidence. This kind of situation often occurs when the plaintiff and the defendant collude with each other maliciously to file sham litigation to help the defendant transfer property and escape debts. Therefore, in practice, even if one party makes self-admission, some judges will continue to inquire about the relevant facts to nip the sham litigation in the bud.

6.4.3 Some Special Circumstances

6.4.3.1 Self-admission Made in Another Case

The self-admission made by the parties in other cases cannot directly produce the legal effect of self-admission in this case. However, if the facts admitted in other cases are recorded in effective judgments, and there is no evidence proving to the contrary, these facts can be directly admitted by the court in this case.

6.4.3.2 Acknowledgment Made in Mediation and Settlement

In the process of mediation presided over by the court and the settlement conducted by the parties themselves, the concessions made by the parties against themselves cannot be regarded as the self-admission of the parties. This is because Chinese law encourages the parties to settle disputes through compromise so as to save time and money for all. It is obvious that the parties will be hesitated to compromise and reach an agreement if the concessions so made will be regarded as a self-admission.

If the settlement is carried out by the parties themselves, we suggest that the parties record the process of the dialogue and make it clear at the beginning that any facts acknowledged during the settlement negotiation shall not be taken as self-admission.

6.4.3.3 Acknowledgment Made on Other Occasions

Some parties will preserve the facts acknowledged by the other party in other occasions than mediation and settlement through audio recording (for secret recording, see Sect. 6.7). This kind of "acknowledgment" obtained secretly can be used as evidence, but it does not have the effect of self-admission. The lawfulness and the probative force of such evidence still need to be determined by the judge in combination with the specific circumstances and other evidence, and the party presenting such evidence generally needs to provide other evidence for corroboration.

6.4.3.4 Self-admission in the Case of Multiple Parties

In the case of multiple plaintiffs/defendants, the effectiveness of the self-admission made by one plaintiff/defendant depends on the nature of the case, i.e., whether it is an ordinary joint action or a necessary joint action.

In the ordinary joint action, the self-admission made by some of the joint litigants is only effective for themselves, but not for other joint litigants. The ordinary joint action refers to a coordinated action instituted by two or more plaintiffs or against two or more defendants in which the subject matter is separable. Such multiple parties are not necessarily required to participate in the court proceedings together. For example, in the equity transfer dispute, if several shareholders sell their equity to the same investor who does not pay the consideration to any shareholder, these shareholders can jointly or individually file a lawsuit against the investor.

By contrast, in the necessary joint action, the self-admission made by some of the joint litigants must be recognized by other joint litigants, otherwise it will not have the effect of self-admission. In the necessary joint action, multiple parties pursue the same subject matter, that is, they have a common and indivisible right and obligation for the legal relationship in dispute, and all obligees or obligors must act as the plaintiff or the defendant collectively. For example, where the creditor lists the debtor and the guarantor as joint defendants, if the guarantor acknowledges the legal relationship agreed in the main contract while the debtor denies it, or vice versa, the acknowledgement will not be deemed as self-admission for both the debtor and the guarantor. Therefore, the court cannot directly determine the existence of the debt relationship agreed in the main contract.

(Reference provisions and information for Sect. 6.4).[4]

---

[4] *Judicial Interpretation of CPL (Revised in 2022): Article 92, 107.*
Judicial Interpretation on Civil Evidence (Revised in 2019): Article 3–9.

6.5 Witness Testimony

The witness testimony is one of the eight types of evidence stipulated by the CPL. In addition to the CPL, relevant judicial interpretations also provide for the witness testimony from various aspects. A witness shall testify in court in principle, but there is no specific provision on cross-examination in Chinese laws. According to Chinese laws, the losing party shall bear the expenses for the witness testimony.

It is worth noting that, the role played by the witness testimony in China's civil litigation is relatively limited for various reasons, and the documentary evidence is still the most important source of evidence. If it is necessary to use the witness testimony, some preparations with the help of lawyers will be needed in most cases.

6.5.1 Who Can Be a Witness

Anyone who knows the circumstances of the case and is able to express his/her thought correctly can be a witness. Even minors and mentally ill persons can testify on issues appropriate to their age and mental status. In practice, the closer the relationship between the witness and the party applying for his/her appearance is, the weaker is the probative force of his/her testimony.

It should be noted that in some countries, the definition of a witness is very broad, and whoever (including the parties concerned) can provide information related to the case can serve as a witness. In China, however, only those other than the parties concerned can be called witnesses. As for the statement of the parties, including the statement of the expert assistant (see Sect. 6.6) engaged by them, it is another type of evidence stipulated by the CPL. Generally speaking, the statement made by the parties against themselves constitute a self-admission (see Sect. 6.4), which has strong probative force; while the statement favoring themselves have very weak probative force.

In addition, although the expert (see Sect. 6.10 for discussion on the examination and appraisal and expert opinions) is not a witness under Chinese law (the expert opinion is another type of evidence different from the witness testimony), the provisions on examining the witness are applicable to the expert as well.

6.5.2 How to Apply for a Witness to Testify in Court

The party concerned shall submit to the court an application for the witness to testify in court before the expiration of the time limit for presenting evidence. The application form shall contain the name, occupation, residence and contact information of the witness, a summary of the testimony, the relevance between the testimony and the facts to be proved, and the necessity of the witness to testify in court. In addition, in cases that might harm national interests and social/public interests, even if the parties do not apply for the witness to testify in court, the court should also summon the relevant witnesses ex officio.

6.5.3 Can a Witness Be Spared Appearing in Court

A witness shall testify in court. Only when the witness suffers from health problems, traffic inconvenience, natural disasters or has other justified reasons, can he/she apply to the court for non-appearance. If the court approves the witness' non-appearance in court, the witness can testify by submitting written testimony, audio and video materials, or by video conference, etc., as appropriate in the opinion of the court.

In cases involving the witness testimony, most judges will require the witnesses to testify in court, otherwise the other party is likely to challenge the effectiveness of the witness's testimony on the grounds that it has not been fully examined.

6.5.4 Does China Have a Cross-Examination System

There is no specific provision on cross-examination in Chinese laws. According to the CPL and relevant judicial interpretations, judges, the parties and their attorneys can question witnesses, but the parties and their attorneys need the permission of judges before questioning witnesses; if judges deem it necessary, they can request witnesses to question each other. However, there are no detailed provisions in Chinese laws on the order, rounds, scope of questions, etc.

In the absence of detailed provisions on the cross-examination, the parties may refer to strategies for questioning witnesses from good examples of cross-examination. However, due to the inquisitorial system of China's civil litigation, any question to witnesses should obtain judges' prior permission. In China's judicial practice, it is the judges who are playing a leading role in the process of litigation and their questioning is often deciding. Therefore, we generally do not recommend our clients to spend too much time in cross-examination strategies.

6.5.5 Who Will Bear the Cost of the Witness Testimony

According to the CPL, the losing party shall bear the expenses for the witness testimony, including the expenses for transportation, accommodation, meals and other necessary expenses for the witness to testify in court, as well as the lost wages. The necessary expenses for transportation, accommodation and meals shall be calculated as per the travel expenses and subsidy standards of the Chinese government's staff; the lost wages shall be calculated as per the average daily wage standard of the workers in the previous year published by the government. Taking Beijing as an example, the subsidy standards are as follows: long-distance transportation is subsidized according to the price of second-class seat of high-speed rail or the economy class flight; CNY 80 per day for urban transportation; CNY 500 per day for accommodation; and CNY 638 per day for lost wages by reference to the average daily wages of Beijing in 2021.

The above economic compensation rules are newly added to the CPL in 2012, to encourage witnesses to testify in court and increase the court appearance rate of witnesses in China's judicial practice. As the recovery of the witness testimony costs often requires the court's involvement, we suggest our clients to actively propose such requests to the court, so as to avoid unnecessary economic losses caused by some judges' unfamiliarity with such rules.

6.5.6 What Is the Effect of Witness Testimony in Practice

Although the law stipulates that it is an obligation to testify in court for those who know the truth, the law does not specify the legal liability of the witness if he/she refuses to do so without justified reasons. In addition, according to a survey about the reasons why witnesses do not testify in court funded by the Chinese Academy of Social Sciences, "averting litigation" and "unwilling to offend others" are the main reasons for many people not wanting to testify in court. This can be confirmed by the statistics from local courts and other studies in this field. According to a statistical report years ago, the rate of Chinese witnesses testifying in court is less than 10%.

Due to the low appearance rate of witnesses, the admission rate of witness testimony has also been greatly affected. In addition, perjury, though being cracked down all the time, never dies in China for various reasons; while the punishment for perjury is relatively low. This further weakens the effectiveness of witness testimony in China's civil litigation.

6.5.7 Conclusions and Suggestions

To sum up, the role of witness testimony in China's civil litigation is relatively limited. If it is necessary to use the witness testimony, our suggestions to the parties are as follows:

(1) The application for witness testimony shall be made before the expiration of the time limit for presenting evidence;
(2) Try the best to persuade the witness to appear in court. If the witness is indeed unable or unwilling to appear in court, try to find justified reasons to persuade the judge to understand the witness' non-appearance;

(3) The witness shall state the specific facts personally experienced by himself/herself, answer questions clearly, and avoid speculations or comments; and
(4) Prepare for the questions that may be raised by the judge and the other party, carefully evaluate the pros and cons of the witness's appearance in court to avoid the adverse effects caused thereby.

(Reference provisions and information for Sect. 6.5).[5]

6.6 Expert Witness in China?—Expert Assistant

Nowadays litigation often involves highly professional issues, which usually go beyond the knowledge of judges, lawyers and the parties themselves. In order to solve these problems, the judge can refer to expert opinions, while the parties can engage expert assistants—or "China's expert witness" as dubbed by some people—to help them express opinions on professional issues.

In practice, expert assistant can contribute to the case in different situations. Although the relevant rules of expert assistant need to be improved, the parties can give it a try to strengthen the persuasion of their opinions.

6.6.1 What Is Expert Assistant?

In terms of professional issues in cases, Chinese judges and the parties have long relied heavily on the impartial third-party, i.e., the expert, in the examination and appraisal (for examination and appraisal, see Sect. 6.10). This has caused some problems: the parties and lawyers, if without the assistance of experts, often find it hard to understand the expert opinions or other professional issues, and therefore have difficulty in effectively expressing targeted opinions. This has resulted in inadequate adversary in the court trial, which is not conducive to the fact-finding.

To solve the above problems, the Judicial Interpretation on Civil Evidence, formulated in 2001, stipulates for the first time that the parties could apply to the court for one or two "persons with expertise" to appear in court, to explain the professional issues of the case, ask the expert questions, and to answer questions of the judges and the parties. This provision was incorporated into the CPL in 2012.

However, "person with expertise" obviously sounds a bit awkward in litigation, so in practice, some might call it "expert witness", as it is similar to the expert witness under the common law system, whereas some others call it "expert assistant", as they think the person with expertise is actually an assistant for the court trial. Given that the opinions of "persons with expertise" are regarded, under Chinese law, as the

---

[5] *CPL (Revised in 2021): Article 66, 75, 76, 77, 142.*
  Judicial Interpretation of CPL (Revised in 2022): Article 102, 117–120, 227, 261.
  Judicial Interpretation on Civil Evidence (Revised in 2019): Article 67–69, 74–76, 96, 99.

statement of the parties rather than the witness testimony, we will refer to them as "expert assistants".

Due to the ambiguous legal provisions on the expert assistant, different courts have different understandings in practice. Some courts regard the expert assistant as a witness and do not allow him/her to participate in the trial; some courts allow the expert assistant to take the seat of the party who has engaged him/her.

6.6.2 Who Can Be the Expert Assistant?

Chinese law does not specify the professional qualification of expert assistants. In theory, as long as the parties believe that someone can explain the professional issues involved clearly, they can apply to the court for the appearance in court of that person as an expert assistant. This is obviously different from the fact that the expert in the examination and appraisal must be selected from the court's expert list. However, in practice, different courts have different approaches. Some courts have a "pool of expert assistants" similar to the list of experts; others review the professional qualification of the candidates proposed by the parties. In addition, some courts even require expert assistants to be an impartial third-party.

To select suitable expert assistants, the parties should better pay attention not only to their professional ability, but also to their expression ability. Also, the parties should help these expert assistants get prepared in advance, which is similar to preparing the witness to appear in court to some extent.

6.6.3 How to Apply for the Expert Assistant to Appear in Court?

The party concerned shall, before the expiration of the time limit for presenting evidence, submit an application to the court, stating the identity of the expert assistant, his/her professional background, and the necessity of appearing in court, etc. Some courts (e.g., Zhejiang High People's Court) allow the parties to apply for the expert and the expert assistant to appear in court together after the expert opinion is made. In practice, there are also cases in which expert assistants are only introduced to appear in court in the second instance.

The expenses for engaging the expert assistant shall be borne by the parties themselves.

6.6.4 What Issues Can the Expert Assistant Express Opinions On?

The Judicial Interpretation on Civil Evidence, as revised in 2019, emphasizes that expert assistants can only express their opinions on expert opinions and professional issues. In practice, typical situations include:

Firstly, only commenting on the expert opinions. For example, in the case of securities-related misrepresentation liability of Founder Technology Group Co., Ltd. in 2019, the judicial expertise institution conducted professional calculation on the investors' losses and the relevance degree with the misrepresentation. Founder Technology Group engaged the expert assistant to express opinions on the calculation.

Secondly, commenting on professional issues in the absence of expert opinions. In the case *Qiong Yao (琼瑶, a famous writer) v. Yu Zheng (于正, a famous playwriter)* for copyright infringement, the plaintiff invited Wang Hailin (汪海林, a famous playwriter) as an expert assistant to express opinions on whether the script in dispute committed plagiarism; the opinions were written into the main text of the judgment by the court, contributing to the plaintiff winning the case.

Thirdly, issuing rebuttal opinions against those of the other party. In the series of cases of *Qihoo 360 v. Tencent* for abusing the dominant market position, both the plaintiff and the defendant engaged expert assistants. In the trial, the expert assistants not only expressed their own opinions, but also refuted the counterpart's opinions. In addition, the court also organized cross examination on expert assistants from both sides. In those cases, the expert assistants exerted a big influence on the judges in the calculation of market share under the Internet environment.

6.6.5 The Effectiveness of the Expert Assistant Opinions in Practice

As mentioned above, due to the vague legal provisions, there is chaos, to a certain degree, regarding the actual operation of the expert assistant system. In addition, expert assistants tend to favor the party engaging them, and sometimes their opinions may thus deviate from scientific facts. These problems make some people look down upon the role of expert assistant and therefore affect the effectiveness of their opinions.

However, with more and more professional issues involved in China's civil litigation, we would still advise our clients to engage expert assistants, to team up with attorneys so as to maximize the advantages of professionals.

6.6.6 Conclusion

Generally speaking, the position of expert assistant in Chinese laws is not clear enough, and the incomplete related rules are far from satisfactory. However, with expert assistants appearing in more and more cases, we believed that this system will be improved. In cases involved with professional issues, we highly advise our clients to engage expert assistants to better tackle problems and persuade judges.

(Reference provisions and information for Sect. 6.6).[6]

6.7 Can Secret Recordings Be Used as Evidence in Chinese Courts?

In China's judicial practice, recording is a common way for collecting evidence. If the secret recording without the permission of the other party satisfies certain conditions, the court may admit it as evidence.

6.7.1 Are Secret Recordings Admissible in Chinese Courts?

There are eight types of evidence stipulated by the CPL, among which the recording evidence is incorporated in Type 4 "audio-visual materials". Therefore, recording falls under the types of evidence permitted by the law.

Although recording can be used as legal evidence, in practice, recording is often made secretly without any awareness of the other party. As for the secret recording, the attitude of Chinese courts has made the shift from negative to positive.

Previously, Chinese courts held that secret recordings were illegal and thus could not be used as evidence at all. However, such a rule excessively limited the means to collect evidence by the parties and therefore had been challenged and criticized by many. In 2001, Chinese courts relaxed the restrictions on secret recording, and admitted its status as evidence *provided that* it neither infringed upon the legitimate rights and interests of others nor violated the prohibitive provisions of the law. By 2015, secret recording can generally be used as evidence unless it "severely" infringes on the legitimate rights and interests of others, violates the prohibitive provisions of the law, or is collected in a way that violates public order and good morals.

---

[6] *CPL (Revised in 2021): Article 82.*
Judicial Interpretation of CPL (Revised in 2022): Article 122, 123.
Judicial Interpretation on Civil Evidence (Revised in 2019): Article 83, 84.
Provisions of the Supreme People's Court on Evidence for Intellectual Property Civil Actions (Fa Shi [2020] No.12): Article 28.
《最高人民法院关于知识产权民事诉讼证据的若干规定》(法释〔2020〕12号).

In addition to the above criteria, some judges have also proposed the following points:

(1) The party concerned shall be present at the time of recording, and it is better that the party himself/herself makes the recording personally;
(2) The secret recording should not be made in the place where recording is prohibited, nor by fraud or coercion; and
(3) Generally speaking, the recording alone cannot be used as the basis for finding the facts, and it must be used together with other evidence to achieve the effect of proof.

6.7.2 What Kind of Recordings Are Unlikely to Be Admitted

According to our experience, in the following situations, the recordings are likely to be dismissed:

(1) If someone submits a recording of a conversation where all the participants have agreed "no recording" at the beginning, the recording of this kind will likely be deemed as illegal for violating the right of privacy;
(2) Where the recording contains fraud and coercion-related contents;
(3) Where the recording is collected in a way that may violate public order and good morals. For example, in a divorce case, one party instigates a kid to talk with the other party and record the conversation secretly;
(4) Where the recording is collected by illegally using professional monitoring equipment;
(5) Where the recording is collected by installing equipment in other's private space (such as bedroom or car);
(6) Where the recording is collected in a place where the same is prohibited (such as in a courtroom); and
(7) Where the recording is collected by hacking into computer or mobile phone through Trojan program.

6.7.3 What Is an Ideal Recording Evidence Like

An ideal recording evidence often has the following characteristics:

(1) The recording should preferably be made by the parties concerned personally;
(2) The basic information of the conversation such as the time, location and the identities of the participants should be clear;
(3) The tone in the conversation should better be calm;
(4) The conversation should better focus on the disputed facts and avoid pointless argument;

(5) The original media (such as recording pen and mobile phone) shall be well preserved; and
(6) If the recording is highly important, it is recommended to engage a notary to notarize the recording process.

Finally, we need to remind that documentary evidence is still the most important evidence in China's judicial practice, while recording evidence is generally used as auxiliary evidence.

(Reference provisions and information for Sect. 6.7).[7]

6.8 How to Collect Evidence from Internet and Social Media

As essentials tool in daily life, the Internet and social media are recognized as sources of evidence by Chinese courts. In ordinary circumstances, the parties can submit hardcopies of contents on the Internet or social media to the court as evidence. However, given that the electronic data generated by the Internet and social media are easy to be tampered with or destroyed, the parties may need to use notarization and other specific methods to ensure the authenticity of electronic evidence.

As a method of evidence collection, notarization has a series of disadvantages, such as costly, not timely, cumbersome for operation and etc. To overcome such disadvantages, some institutions began to provide evidence collection service by timestamp. In practice, evidence collection by timestamp has been widely recognized by Chinese courts, and the costs are quite low, so that the parties can make full use of it. Based on the timestamp, the evidence collection by blockchain enhances the credibility of timestamp by using blockchain technology. Chinese courts have recognized blockchain as a method of evidence collection and are strengthening the research on it.

6.8.1 Basic Methods of Collecting Evidence from Internet and Social Media

The electronic data generated from the Internet and social media (including email) is one of the eight types of evidence recognized by the CPL. The hard copies or other displayable and identifiable output media submitted by the parties consistent with

---

[7] *CPL (Revised in 2021): Article 66.*
  Judicial Interpretation of CPL (Revised in 2022): Article 106.
  Reply of the Supreme People's Court on the Inadmissibility of the Data Obtained by Recording the Conversation Without the Consent of the Other Party (Fa Fu [1995] No. 2).
  《最高人民法院关于未经对方当事人同意私自录制其谈话取得的资料不能作为证据使用的批复》(法复〔1995〕2号).

the electronic data are deemed as the original electronic data. Therefore, in practice, the parties would usually print a hard copy of e-mails, webpages and etc. and submit the same to the court.

However, given the very nature of digital evidence being easily tampered with and destroyed, Chinese courts are highly concerned about the authenticity of such evidence. What Chinese courts review mainly focus on:

(1) Whether the software/hardware system where the content is generated, collected, stored and transmitted is safe and reliable;
(2) Whether the storage and safekeeping media are definite, and whether the safekeeping methods and means are appropriate;
(3) Whether the content is clear and complete, and whether the content is added, deleted or modified; and
(4) Whether the content can be verified through a specific form.

6.8.2 Strengthen the Weight of Evidence by Notarization

To deal with the above issues of electronic data, it is considerable for the parties to collect evidence by notarization, so as to strengthen the weight of evidence and rise to the challenge from the opposite parties.

Notarization is the activity of proving certain facts and documents. In China, the notarization function is exercised by the notary office established by the government, and the specific work is carried out by the full-time notary employed by the notary office. According to China's evidence rules, the notarial certificate issued by the notary office has stronger probative force than the general evidence. Therefore, for crucial evidence, it is necessary to collect evidence by notarization.

As to the e-mail, the parties may check their own e-mail on the computer of the notary office, and the notary shall confirm the existence and content of the e-mail. Although this kind of notarization cannot prove the entire process from e-mail generation to sending (or receiving), and there is also the possibility that the parties forge the e-mail for notarization, the court shall confirm the authenticity of the notarized e-mail, unless the other party can present evidence proving the contrary.

As to the contents of webpages and social media, the parties may check them on the computers and mobile phones of the notary office, and the notary shall confirm that such contents exist on the Internet at a certain time point, save the same by printing or recording a CD, and issue a notarial certificate therefore.

Compared with other emerging evidence collection methods, the cost of notarization is higher; besides, it is difficult to achieve real-time evidence collection due to the need to make appointments with notaries in advance. Nevertheless, given the strongest credibility that notarization enjoys, the notarized evidence is very unlikely to be overthrown by the court.

6.8.3 Evidence Collection by Timestamp

6.8.3.1 What Is the Principle of Evidence Collection and Verification by Timestamp

The timestamp is an electronic certificate issued by the timestamp service institution to prove that the electronic data have existed at a certain time point, and are complete and verifiable. The timestamp issued by an authoritative neutral institution can be recognized by Chinese courts, and therefore is legally effective.

The basic principle of evidence collection and verification by timestamp: the party uploads the hash value obtained by hashing the electronic data to the timestamp service institution, which will encrypt the hash value and the uploading time, and provide the encrypted data in the form of an electronic document (i.e., the timestamp) to the party.

Since the hash value of any electronic data is unique, so is the content of each timestamp. If the electronic data with a timestamp submitted by the party is challenged by the other side, the party concerned may ask the timestamp service institution for decryption. If the hash value and generation time of the evidence read after decryption is consistent with the evidence itself, it is enough to prove that the evidence has not been tampered with.

In addition, because the hash algorithm is irreversible, the timestamp service institution cannot obtain the specific content of the electronic data by reverse calculation according to the hash value uploaded by the user. Therefore, the evidence collection by timestamp is also highly confidential.

6.8.3.2 Which Timestamp Institutions Are Recognized by Chinese Courts

In judicial practice, UniTrust Time Stamp Authority (联合信任时间戳服务中心, https://www.tsa.cn/) is the most commonly used and highly recognized timestamp service institution. As UniTrust Time Stamp Authority cooperates with the National Time Service Center of the Chinese Academy of Sciences, the only statutory time service institution in China, the timestamps issued by it are widely recognized by courts at all levels. In addition, the Copyright Association of Guangzhou (http://www.cagz.org/), Shenzhen Copyright Society (http://www.scs.org.cn/) and other organizations also have in-depth cooperation with UniTrust for timestamp services in local areas, and the timestamps produced by such organizations can also be recognized by Chinese courts.

6.8.3.3 Pros and Cons of Evidence Collection by Timestamp

Taking UniTrust Time Stamp Authority as an example, the operation platform is available 24/7, and all operations can be completed by the parties themselves. For static web pages, the platform provides one-click evidence collection. The standard rate of one timestamp is only CNY 10. Therefore, for static web pages, the timestamp is a convenient, fast and low-cost way to obtain evidence.

However, for web pages with dynamic pictures or videos, web pages that require login, web pop-ups and mobile phone APPs, the one-click evidence collection may fail to wholly collect the contents. Under such circumstances, the parties need to use more expensive functions, such as screen recording evidence collection. In some extreme situations, the parties need to design a strict process by themselves, starting from the cleanliness inspection of equipment and network, operating manually throughout the whole process, and applying for timestamps for the results of each step. Therefore, it is not that easy to use the timestamp to obtain evidence in complex forms. Once there is any omission in any step, the effectiveness of evidence may be challenged.

In addition, if the content proved by the timestamp is different from that of the notarial certificate, some courts hold that the notarial certificate shall prevail.

6.8.4 Evidence Collection by Blockchain

6.8.4.1 What Is the Principle of Evidence Collection and Verification by Blockchain?

Based on the timestamp, the evidence collection by blockchain enhances the credibility of timestamp by using blockchain technology. The principles of evidence collection and verification by blockchain are as follows: the parties upload the electronic data to the network platform of the blockchain institution, which will make the timestamp of the electronic data, and then store the copies thereof in the servers of other cooperation platforms. Under the constraint of the blockchain consensus mechanism, any change to the timestamp needs to be agreed and recorded by each platform, and no platform can tamper with the timestamp alone. As a result, the probative force of timestamps has been further increased through the blockchain technology.

It is worth noting that the three existing Internet courts in China have taken themselves as a node on the chain and cooperated with different blockchain institutions to build their own blockchain verification system. Taking "Balance Chain" (天平链) established by Beijing Internet Court as an example, the parties may require the blockchain platform to store the electronic data and its hash value on "Balance Chain", which will issue the corresponding verification number to the parties. As long as the parties submit the verification number and the original electronic data, the Internet court can automatically verify the authenticity and the generation time of

6.8 How to Collect Evidence from Internet and Social Media

the electronic data in the backstage. In addition to "Balance Chain", "Alliance Chain" (联盟链) developed by Ant Blockchain (蚂蚁区块链) and accessed by Hangzhou Internet Court, and "Internet Legal Chain" (网通法链) established by Guangzhou Internet Court also have such functions. This has greatly improved the efficiency of evidence examination.

Based on the successful experience of blockchain verification of Internet courts, some local courts have also established blockchain verification systems. At present, the SPC is also establishing a "Judicial Chain" (司法链) for courts nationwide. It is believed that the evidence collection by blockchain can be more widely used in Chinese courts in the future.

6.8.4.2 Advantages of Evidence Collection by Blockchain

As is the case in the evidence collection by timestamp, the evidence collection by blockchain is also affordable and convenient. Many blockchain platforms have developed self-help evidence collection functions. For example, on "BaoQuan.com" (保全网) (https://www.baoquan.com/), the parties can take a screenshot of the web page or record the computer operation process through this website, and upload it to the network service platform to obtain the corresponding "preservation number" and evidence data package for future verification. The standard rate for one web page evidence collection is CNY 5. For screen recording or computer operation process recording, the rate is CNY 50/10 min, and CNY 5/min for each extra minute. In addition, the party concerned can also apply for the judicial authentication certificate issued by the institution of judicial appraisal and examination through the website at the same time of obtaining evidence, and the certificate will explain the process and method of obtaining evidence, the cleanliness of the environment for obtaining evidence, etc. The judicial authentication certificate is helpful to further strengthen the effectiveness of evidence collection.

At present, the commonly used blockchain service institutions include, inter alia, "BaoQuan.com" cooperating with Hangzhou Internet Court and "TRUSTDO" (信任度) cooperating with Beijing Internet Court.

6.8.4.3 Limitations of Evidence Collection by Blockchain

Technically, evidence collection by blockchain can only ensure that the data cannot be tampered with and deleted after being stored on the chain. If the data are "fake" before being stored, such data actually has no credibility. Although there have been many cases in which evidence collected by blockchain was admitted by courts, this evidence collection method still needs to stand the test of time.

(Reference provisions and information for Sect. 6.8).[8]

---

[8] *CPL (Revised in 2021): Article 66.*
Judicial Interpretation of CPL (Revised in 2022): Article 93, 116.

6.9 Technical Examination Officer

Technical examination officer is a trial assistant to assist the judge in finding out technical facts of the case. Like the expert in the examination and appraisal, the technical examination officer is a neutral third party but has closer communication with judges, which also reduces judges' dependence on the examination and appraisal.

In practice, the technical examination officer not only assists the judge in finding out technical facts, but also contributes to promoting the efficiency and controlling the cost for litigation. Although the technical examination officer system is still young, we believe that it will play a bigger role in the future.

6.9.1 What Is Technical Examination Officer

The core of technology-related intellectual property case trial is to find out and determine the technical facts. Because judges often lack relevant expertise, they rely heavily on the examination and appraisal (for examination and appraisal, see Sect. 6.10). However, the technical examination is often time-consuming and costly, and will bring out the problem of "substituting examination for trial" (以鉴代审).

In order to solve the above problems, on 31 Dec. 2014, China piloted the technical examination officer system in three intellectual property courts in Beijing, Shanghai and Guangzhou. Combining the experiences of the three courts, in May 2019, the SPC issued the Provisions of the Supreme People's Court on the Participation of Technical Examination Officers in Intellectual Property Litigation (最高人民法院关于技术调查官参与知识产权案件诉讼活动的若干规定, hereinafter referred to as the "Provisions on TEO"), expanding the application scope of the system to all civil, administrative and criminal cases related to intellectual property heard by courts nationwide.

According to the Provisions on TEO, the technical examination officer is a trial assistant who provides the judge with technical examination advice, but has no right to decide the result of the judgment. The technical examination officer may participate in such activities as evidence collection, investigation, preservation, pretrial conference, court hearing and post-trial deliberation of the case, and shall, with the consent of the judge, have the right to question the parties, experts, witnesses and other litigation participants on the technical issues involved in the case. The technical examination officer may also provide technical advice to judges without participating in the abovementioned activities.

It depends on the judge to decide whether the technical examination officer should participate in a case. A judge may apply to his court or the court at a higher level

---

Judicial Interpretation on Civil Evidence (Revised in 2019): Article 14, 15, 94.
Provisions of the Supreme People's Court on Several Issues Concerning the Hearing of Cases by Internet Courts (Fa Shi [2018] No.16): Article 11.
《最高人民法院关于互联网法院审理案件若干问题的规定》(法释〔2018〕16号).

for the assignment of a technical examination officer. Apart from applying for the recusal of the technical examination officer, the law does not give the parties the right to express other opinions.

6.9.2 Who Can Be the Technical Examination Officer

It is obvious that a technical examination officer appointed by the court must have expertise in a particular area. At present, the sources of technical examination officers are relatively diverse, which can be roughly divided into the following categories:

(1) Teachers from universities and other professionals on a part-time basis;
(2) Professionals seconded from the intellectual property bureaus and other government agencies on a full-time basis, and they will return to their original work upon the expiration of the secondment period; and
(3) Full-time technical examination officers engaged by the court.

In general, local courts will prepare their rosters of technical examination officers. In November 2019, the Intellectual Property Court of the SPC established the "National Technical Examination Officer Pool" and the "National Technical Examination Officer Sharing Mechanism". This makes it possible for courts nationwide to share technical examination officers, making up for the understaff and the inadequate expertise of technical examination officers in some local courts.

6.9.3 Effectiveness of the Opinion of the Technical Examination Officer

The advisory opinion of the technical examination officer on the technical facts involved in the case is a reference for the judge to determine the technical facts, and the authority to determine the facts is still vested in the judge. As an internal opinion for the judge's reference, this advisory opinion is not a type of evidence stipulated by the law, nor open to the parties, and therefore the parties have no right to examine the same.

However, if a technical examination officer participates in the case trial, the parties have the right to express their own opinions on his/her actions and opinions in the trial.

6.9.4 How Does the Technical Examination Officer System Work

Like the experts in examination and appraisal, technical examination officers take a neutral standing. Given that the examination and appraisal is time-consuming and costly, the establishment of the technical examination officer system, to a large extent, has reduced the judge's dependence on the former. Some court has taken a case involving source code comparison of computer software as an example to illustrate that: the examination fee is charged according to the number of codes, and the general software has thousands of lines of codes, so it will cost several hundred thousands yuan, and also a period of time ranging from a few months to many years. In order to save time and money, the court, after seeking the opinions of both parties, appoints a technical examination officer to use professional software to conduct a comparison with the participation of both parties, and the final result is acceptable to all. This practice has greatly improved trial efficiency.

If the examination is necessary for the case, the technical examination officer can assist the judge in determining the matters and scope of the examination. During the court trial, the technical examination officer can also help judges to review the expert opinion and the opinions of expert assistants of both parties, so as to help judges handle conflicting expert opinions.

In addition to the technical examination officer, some courts also introduce people's assessor with expertise or consult experts for finding out technical facts. However, these practices have not been fully promoted due to lack of related mechanisms and inefficiency. In contrast, although the technical examination officer system is still young, it has gathered a wealth of experience. We believe that the technical examination officer system will play a bigger role in intellectual property cases.

(Reference provisions and information for Sect. 6.9).[9]

6.10 Expert Opinions—Professional Opinions Provided by Neutral Judicial Expertise Institutions

The expert opinion ("鉴定意见" in Chinese) is professional opinions provided by a neutral judicial expertise institution to the court on some factual issues of a case. The expert opinion is one of the eight types of statutory evidence stipulated by the CPL, and therefore plays an important role in China's civil litigation.

Expert opinions have been heavily weighted by judges for a long time, and the practice of "substituting case trial by appraisal or examination" can be frequently

---

[9] *Judicial Interpretation on Civil Evidence (Revised in 2019): Article 84.*

Provisions of the Supreme People's Court on the Participation of Technical Examination Officers in Intellectual Property Litigation (Fa Shi [2019] No.2): Article 1–14.

《最高人民法院关于技术调查官参与知识产权案件诉讼活动的若干规定》(法释〔2019〕2号).

witnessed. Although Chinese courts are trying to reverse such practice, expert opinions will still play a very important role in the judge's decision making. The costs of appraisal and examination are generally borne by the losing party.

6.10.1 What Is Expert Opinion

Expert opinion is, under the entrustment of the court, the opinion provided by the designated judicial expertise institution on the professional factual issues of a case. It is an important reference for the fact-finding by the judge. The expert opinion should only be about the facts of the case, and the application of law can only be determined by the judge.

In practice, the most common professional issues are technical problems, such as the authenticity of the signature, the causality between environmental pollution and pollution discharge, the paternity testing, etc., and value appraisal, such as the evaluation of project cost in construction projects.

We will only discuss the expert opinion of court-appointed judicial expertise institutions here. In addition to that, the parties may also entrust judicial expertise institutions for expert opinions, which, however, would generally not be admitted by the court once being questioned by the other party.

6.10.2 Who Can Be the Expert

The judicial expertise institution shall be selected from the list compiled by the court. Local courts will compile their own lists of judicial expertise institutions, most of which are local. Therefore, which judicial expertise institutions you can choose from depends on the court before which you bring a lawsuit.

The list of judicial expertise institutions is classified by types. In China, expertise institutions in their respective areas would generally obtain accreditation from administrative authorities or industry associations, which sets a key reference for local courts to make their list of judicial expertise institutions accordingly. For example, the Ministry of Justice and its local government counterparts will register and make a list of judicial expertise institutions for forensic, physical evidence, audio-visual data and environmental damage; the Ministry of Housing and Urban–Rural Development and the corresponding functional departments of local governments will grant accreditation to project cost evaluation institutions. Generally, the court will select from these qualified institutions and make their final list of judicial expertise institutions.

After the judicial expertise institution is determined, the expert shall be appointed by the institution. The parties have the right to apply for the recusal of the expert.

6.10.3 How to Initiate the Appraisal and Examination

Generally speaking, the appraisal and examination (or authentication) is initiated by the parties' application. The parties may apply to the court within the time limit of presenting evidence, and the appraisal and examination will start upon examination and approval of the court. The court will mainly review the relevance between the matters to be appraised or examined and the facts to be proved, as well as the evidential significance to the facts to be proved.

In addition, when the court deems it necessary to ask for expert opinions, but neither party has submitted the application, the court is entitled to initiate the appraisal and examination ex officio. However, in practice, considering the costs and other issues, the court will generally not take the initiative. Instead, the court will prompt the parties to do so by informing their right to apply for appraisal and examination and the disadvantages of abandoning such right.

6.10.4 How to Select the Expert

After the court allows the application, it will select a judicial expertise institution randomly from the list by drawing lots or computer lottery. The parties may also agree on one judicial expertise institution from the list. However, it is difficult for both parties to reach a consensus in practice, so under most circumstances, the institution is randomly selected by the court.

The selection method makes the judicial expertise institution and the expert a neutral third-party to the parties of the case. In contrast, the expert assistant in China (for expert assistant, see Sect. 6.6) is engaged by and acts on behalf of one party only.

6.10.5 What Is the Effect of Expert Opinion

Expert opinions are generally heavily weighted by judges, owing to the neutrality of judicial expertise institutions and experts, and the fact that judges often lack professional abilities on matters to be appraised or examined (or authenticated). The expert opinion used to be called "the expert conclusion" (鉴定结论) in the CPL before its 2012 revision, and had a higher probative force than that of other documentary evidence. At that time, some judges relied too heavily on expert opinions to make decisions, and even left legal issues to judicial expertise institutions. For example, in medical malpractice tort cases, some judges let the experts make conclusion on whether the medical institution commits "fault". However, "fault" is the subjective evaluation of medical staff, which is a typical legal issue and should be determined by the judge himself/herself.

In order to reverse this erroneous practice of "substituting case trial by appraisal or examination" (以鉴代审), the provisions stipulating that the expert opinion has a higher probative force have been canceled in Chinese laws. In 2014, the SPC also issued Guiding Case No. 24 to remind judges to distinguish between factual and legal issues and not to rely entirely on expert opinions.

Case No. 24 was about a traffic accident that occurred in Jiangsu Province. The plaintiff sued to recover the damages sustained by him in consequence of being knocked down on the crosswalk by a car of the defendant. The judicial expertise institution held that the osteoporosis had contributed 25% to the plaintiff's disability. Therefore, the court of first instance reduced the plaintiff's disability compensation by 25% according to the expert opinion. The court of second instance overturned the first-instance judgment on the grounds that the premise of deducting disability compensation was that the plaintiff had committed a fault in the legal sense to the accident; although the plaintiff's physical condition had a certain impact on the damages, the plaintiff himself committed no fault in the legal sense. Therefore, it was erroneous for the court of first instance to deduct the plaintiff's disability compensation according to the expert opinion.

While weakening the role of expert opinion, the right of the parties to challenge the expert opinion has been strengthened in Chinese laws. If the parties have objections to the expert opinion, they may require the expert to appear in court for examination and engage an expert assistant to ask questions. If the expert refuses to appear in court without justified reasons, the judge shall not take the expert opinion so made as the basis for the final decision.

It should be noted that although the role of expert opinion has been weakened, it still plays a very important role in the judge's decision making, especially in the cases when it is difficult to distinguish factual issues from legal issues. We highly recommend that the parties take the expert opinion seriously, and if necessary, engage an expert assistant to examine the expert opinion.

6.10.6 Costs of Appraisal and Examination

The costs of appraisal and examination (or authentication) vary from different matters and locations of the institutions. For the appraisal and examination of forensic, physical evidence and audio-visual materials, it will be the judicial administrative departments of provincial governments to set the unified price. For other matters, the parties should better first check if there is a price set by the government. If not, the parties can only make a deal with the expertise institutions, which are at an obvious advantage though.

Generally, the costs of appraisal and examination shall be prepaid by the applicant, and finally borne by the losing party.

(Reference provisions and information for Sect. 6.10).[10]

---

[10] *CPL (Revised in 2021): Article 79–82.*

6.11 Evidence Investigation and Collection by the Court—A Complement to the Presentation of Evidence by the Parties Themselves

"The burden of proof lies with the party asserting a proposition" is a primary rule in the judicial proceedings. However, the parties' means and ability to collect evidence are limited. Therefore, Chinese laws stipulate that the court can investigate and collect evidence under certain circumstances.

6.11.1 What Evidence Can Be Investigated and Collected by the Court

When the evidence is held by a third party, especially the relevant government departments, and is difficult for the parties to obtain, the parties can apply to the court for evidence investigation and collection. In practice, some typical examples of this kind of evidence include:

(1) Data kept by government departments. For example, the land and housing registration files, the complete company files kept by the company registration authority, and the administrative approval documents not made publicly available;
(2) Files and materials of other related cases under the possession of the court;
(3) Deposit and withdrawal slips and transaction records held by financial institutions (third-party payment platforms); and
(4) Other types of evidence involving state secrets, business secrets or personal privacy. For example, records of goods received and shipped by ports and shipping companies (not parties to the case), personal travel and communication records.

In addition to the application by the parties, the court can investigate and collect evidence ex officio under specific circumstances. However, in practice, it is rare that the court takes the initiative to collect evidence. In most cases, the court will only do so by the application of the parties.

Judicial Interpretation of CPL (Revised in 2022): Article 121.
Judicial Interpretation on Civil Evidence (Revised in 2019): Article 30–32, 36–41.
Notice of the Supreme People's Court on Printing and Distributing the Implementation Measures for the Expert Witness Roster System of People's Courts (Fa Fa [2004] No.6): Article 16, 18.
《最高人民法院关于印发 < 人民法院司法鉴定人名册制度实施办法 > 的通知》*(法发〔2004〕6号).*

6.11.2 How to Apply to the Court for Evidence Investigation and Collection

The parties shall submit an application to the court prior to the expiration of the time limit for presenting evidence, specifying the particulars of the person being investigated, the to-be-collected evidence and the to-be-proved facts, as well as providing clear clues thereof (such as the bank account number, the possible location of the evidence and other information).

6.11.3 How Does the Court Investigate and Collect Evidence

First of all, the application needs to be approved by the court. In reviewing such applications, the court will mainly consider:

(1) Whether the evidence in question is really impossible for the parties to collect for objective reasons; and
(2) Whether the evidence in question is related to and significant for the to-be-proved facts.

If the court allows the application, it shall assign at least two court personnel to the person being investigated for evidence collection, generally on site, and the court personnel shall strictly preserve the evidence and record the collecting process. In the court trial, such evidence shall be displayed to the parties concerned for examination.

Due to the lack of resources and personnel, and in order to improve the efficiency of evidence collection, the "Lawyer Investigation Order" (律师调查令) has come into being in the judicial practice. In this regard, after the parties apply to the court for evidence collection, the court may issue an investigation order, with which the lawyer is authorized to collect evidence from the person being investigated. This means that the court authorizes part of the investigation power to the attorney of the party concerned, which facilitates the evidence collection of the party concerned or the attorney. The Lawyer Investigation Order has been quite common in the practice of courts in various regions. However, this system is still in the exploratory and trial stage, and is in want of unified provisions applicable nationwide. In practice, some persons being investigated will disregard the Lawyer Investigation Order and require the court personnel to be present in person for evidence investigation and collection.

6.11.4 The Probative Force of the Evidence Collected by Courts

The evidence collected by courts shall be deemed as the evidence submitted by the applicant, and shall still be subject to the evidence examination procedure. The evidence collected by courts ex officio generally needs to be presented during the court trial. The court shall give explanations on the evidence collection and consider opinions of both parties on the probative force.

It is worth noting that the application for evidence collection by the court can only serve as a complement to the presentation of evidence by the parties themselves, and it does not work all the time. If the application is dismissed, the parties still need to bear the adverse consequences arising out of failure to present evidence. Therefore, both the plaintiff and the defendant should properly maintain operation documents and materials in their daily work, and try their best to collect the evidence at hand in case of litigation, rather than relying on the court for evidence collection.

(Reference provisions and information for Sect. 6.11).[11]

6.12 How Do Chinese Courts Assist Foreign Courts in Investigation and Evidence Collection

According to the Convention on the Taking of Evidence Abroad in Civil or Commercial Matters (hereinafter referred to as the "Hague Evidence Taking Convention") and the bilateral treaties signed by China, Chinese courts are obligated to assist foreign courts in investigation and evidence collection. The specific handling process is quite similar to that of assisting foreign courts in serving court documents. However, Chinese courts also set certain requirements on the relevance between the target evidence and the foreign case. In addition, the matters for which foreign courts request assistance shall not undermine China's sovereignty and security.

6.12.1 Assistance in Investigation and Evidence Collection Under the Hague Evidence Taking Convention

Given that China is a contracting state to the Hague Evidence Taking Convention, Chinese courts shall, as per certain procedures, handle the requests for assistance in investigation and evidence collection made by other contracting states according to the Hague Evidence Taking Convention. This process is quite similar to the service of foreign court documents in China according to the Convention on the Service Abroad of Judicial and Extrajudicial Documents in Civil or Commercial Matters, namely:

(1) The Central Authority of the requesting state submits the paperwork to the Ministry of Justice of the People's Republic of China (the Central Authority designated by the Chinese government);

---

[11] *CPL (Revised in 2021): Article 67.*
Judicial Interpretation of CPL (Revised in 2022): Article 94–97.
Judicial Interpretation on Civil Evidence (Revised in 2019): Article 2, 20–24.

(2) The Ministry of Justice forwards the paperwork to the SPC;
(3) After examining the integrity of the paperwork and confirming that there are no grounds for refusal, the SPC forwards the paperwork to the high court of the place where the evidence or the witness is located;
(4) The high court may either further forwards the paperwork to the intermediate or primary court to handle the matter, or handle the matter on its own;
(5) After the paperwork is checked as error-free and the requested investigation or evidence collection has been completed, the result shall be returned to the Ministry of Justice according to the original route; and
(6) The Ministry of Justice submits the paperwork to the Central Authority of the requesting state, thus completing all the procedures for assistance in investigation or evidence collection.

According to Article 9 of the Hague Evidence Taking Convention, Chinese courts may follow a request of the requesting state that a special method or procedure be followed, unless this is incompatible with the Chinese law or impossible of performance by reason of practical difficulties. In the absence of special request from the requesting state, the Chinese court will assist in the investigation and evidence collection in accordance with the methods and procedures prescribed by the Chinese law. In practice, the common methods of investigation and evidence collection by Chinese courts include, among other things, obtaining files and questioning witnesses. In a case involving paternity testing, a Shanghai court also assisted a Swiss court in extracting DNA samples from a child.

Chinese courts also set certain requirements on the scope of investigation and evidence collection. At the time of accession to the Hague Evidence Taking Convention, China declared, in accordance with Article 23 thereof, that for requests from common-law countries for pre-trial discovery, only those documents listed in the request and directly and closely related to the case would be executed.

In addition, if the results of investigation and evidence collection, upon their publication, will damage China's sovereignty and security, or may disclose state secrets or infringe trade secrets, Chinese courts will refuse to provide such results.

Finally, it should be noted that, in principle, China does not allow courts of the requesting state to investigate and collect evidence on their own in China. The only exception is that, according to Article 15 of the Hague Evidence Taking Convention, the court of the requesting state may collect evidence from its citizens through its diplomatic or consular officials in China, but may not take compulsory measures during this process.

6.12.2 Assistance in Investigation and Evidence Collection Under Bilateral Treaties

In addition to assistance in service, most of the bilateral judicial assistance treaties in civil or commercial matters concluded by China also concern assistance in investigation and evidence collection. When assisting the contracting parties to both the Hague Evidence Taking Convention and bilateral treaties on investigation and evidence collection, Chinese courts may provide assistance based on either of the two legal grounds as the case may be. Besides, the principle of reciprocity also applies in this context.

(Reference provisions and information for Sect. 6.12).[12]

6.13 Evidence Preservation—The Court's Preservation of Evidence that May Be Destroyed

When the evidence may be destroyed or difficult to be collected in the future, the court can investigate, collect and preserve the evidence ex officio or upon the application of the parties. This is the Evidence Preservation System. It is different from, at the same time overlaps with the evidence investigation and collection system.

The evidence preservation usually catches the other party unprepared, and therefore is generally favorable to the applicant. However, there are some difficulties in its practical operation, so the court will usually be prudent to approve it.

6.13.1 What Is Evidence Preservation

Evidence preservation is a measure taken by the court to investigate, collect and preserve the evidence when it may be destroyed or difficult to be collected in the future. The specific measures include, inter alia, taking photos of, duplicating and detaining the evidence. In practice, evidence preservation is used when the evidence

---

[12] *Provisions of the Supreme People's Court on Judicial Assistance Requests for Service of Judicial Documents and Investigation and Evidence Collection in Handling Civil and Commercial Cases under International Conventions and Bilateral Judicial Assistance Treaties (Revised in 2020, Fa Shi [2013] No.11).*

《最高人民法院关于依据国际公约和双边司法协助条约办理民商事案件司法文书送达和调查取证司法协助请求的规定》(2020年修订, 法释〔2013〕11号).

Notice of the Supreme People's Court on Promulgation of "Implementing Rules for Provisions on Requesting Judicial Assistance in Service of Documents and Evidence Collection in Accordance with International Conventions and Bilateral Judicial Assistance Treaties (for Trial Implementation)" (Fa Fa [2013] No.6).

《最高人民法院印发 <关于依据国际公约和双边司法协助条约办理民商事案件司法文书送达和调查取证司法协助请求的规定实施细则(试行)> 的通知》(法发[2013]6号).

is controlled by the other party and may be tampered with or destroyed at any time. The parties can apply to the court for preserving the following evidence:

(1) Evidence under the control of the other party and may be destroyed at any time, such as the alleged infringing products, programs, drawings and technical data subject to alleged infringement saved in computers and data storage units;
(2) Evidence that cannot be moved or is difficult to be preserved, such as, large mechanical equipment, buildings, vehicles and perishable commodities; and
(3) Evidence involving state secrets, personal privacy and business secrets, etc.

The intellectual property cases are where the evidence preservation system plays very important role. In such cases, the evidence of infringement and profits obtained by infringement is generally in the hands of infringers. It is hard for the right holder to have access to such evidence, let alone to preserve the same. Therefore, the chance of winning often relies on evidence preservation.

China's notary office also provides a service called "notarization of evidence preservation"(证据保全公证), but this service only notarizes the process of the evidence collection, to confirm that the evidence has not been tampered with. Therefore, though with a similar name, it is totally different from the "evidence preservation" by the court.

6.13.2 Comparison Between Evidence Preservation and Evidence Investigation and Collection by Courts

Both mechanisms can help the parties collect evidence that is hard to do by themselves. However, evidence preservation mainly focuses on preserving evidence that may be destroyed for subjective and objective reasons. For example, due to its own material, the evidence may perish or deteriorate, or the respondent may deliberately damage the evidence, etc. By contrast, evidence investigation and collection by courts focuses more on helping the parties get evidence, which, though not likely to be destroyed, is difficult for them to do so by themselves for objective reasons. For example, the evidence is controlled by a third party (especially the government department), such as the export declaration form or the land and housing registration files.

6.13.3 Application and Examination of Evidence Preservation

In terms of the commencement of proceedings, the same with the evidence investigation and collection by courts, the evidence preservation is initiated mainly by application, and sometimes by the court ex officio under special circumstances. The parties shall, prior to the expiration of the time limit for presenting evidence, apply in writing to the court for evidence preservation, indicating, inter alia, the particulars of the evidence to be preserved, the reasons for the application and the preservation measures to be taken.

Under emergent circumstances where the evidence may be destroyed if the preservation measures are not taken immediately, the parties may apply for evidence preservation before the case filing. In this case, the parties should, in addition to the aforementioned matters, prove their interest with the preservation objects, and state the necessity of the immediate preservation measures. Once the court takes preservation measures therefor, the parties need to file a lawsuit within one month, otherwise the preservation measures will be lifted.

When examining the application of evidence preservation, the court mainly reviews the applicant's qualification, the possibility of the evidence being destroyed or difficulty to collect in the future, the relevance between the evidence to be preserved and the facts to be proved. If the preservation measures may cause losses to the evidence holder, the court will require the applicant to provide certain guarantee.

In practice, the applicant of evidence preservation needs to provide the court with detailed clues about the evidence to be preserved, such as its content and location, how to enter the place, and communicate with the court in advance on how to implement preservation measures. Given that preservation measures will consume many resources of the court, and may cause a certain degree of antagonism and danger, the court generally reviews the application with prudence.

6.13.4 The Method and Effect of Evidence Preservation

If the application for evidence preservation is approved, the court will choose preservation measures that have the least impact on the interests of evidence holder. Common preservation measures include photographing, video recording, sampling, sealing up and seizing. When it is possible to preserve evidence by photographing, measures such as sealing up and seizing shall not be taken in principle; for the evidence preserved by such severe measures, an inspection therefor shall be conducted in a timely manner.

If the parties do not cooperate with or even obstruct evidence preservation by the court, they may be fined or detained. If the court already has the prima facie evidence in the process of evidence preservation, and the parties obstruct further evidence preservation, it may be deemed as obstructing evidence presentation. The court may presume that the claim made by the applicant is established according to the facts already known.

The preserved evidence has the same effect as the evidence investigated and collected by the court in judicial proceedings. The preserved evidence will be seen as evidence provided by the applicant, and shall be subject to the evidence examination procedure; the evidence preserved by the court ex officio shall be presented in court and the opinions of the parties shall be heard.

6.14 Evidence Discovery and Disclosure in China?—Evidence Presentation Order

(Reference provisions and information for Sect. 6.13).[13]

6.14 Evidence Discovery and Disclosure in China?—Evidence Presentation Order

In cases where the evidence is completely controlled by one party and the other party has no way to collect, unfairness judgments may arise. To solve this problem, China has gradually set up the evidence presentation order system. Given it is designed to force the evidence controller to provide the evidence, some people call it China's "evidence discovery and disclosure" system. However, there is a marked difference between the two.

The evidence presentation order is a young mechanism, and the specific rules thereof need further improvement. Still, in addition to collecting evidence by themselves, the parties may actively employ this system.

6.14.1 What Is Evidence Presentation Order

Generally speaking, neither party will submit evidence against themselves in a lawsuit. If the key evidence is completely controlled by one party, and the other party has no way to obtain and submit the same to the court, the judgment will very much likely to be an unfair one. For a long time, there was no such mechanism in the Chinese law to solve this problem, which is particularly prominent in determining the profits obtained by the infringer in IP infringement cases.

To tackle this problem, when China revised its Trademark Law in 2013, a provision that the court may order the infringer to provide financial books was added. After that, the SPC extended the scope of application of the above practices to all documentary evidence, audio-visual materials and electronic data. The party concerned may claim that the evidence in question is in the hands of the other party, and apply to the court to order the other party to submit the same; if the court approves the application, but the other party refuses to do so, the court may presume that the evidence claimed by the applicant is true. If the other party destroys the evidence in question, the court may impose a fine and/or detention on it. It is worth noting that even if the evidence involves state secrets, trade secrets and privacy, the party concerned can still be required to submit such evidence, provided that the examination of the same is not conducted publicly.

---

[13] *CPL (Revised in 2021): Article 84.*
Judicial Interpretation of CPL (Revised in 2022): Article 98.
Judicial Interpretation on Civil Evidence (Revised in 2019): Article 25–29.

6.14.2 Is China's Evidence Presentation Order Equal to the Evidence Discovery and Disclosure?

Viewed from the purpose of the system, some would call the evidence presentation order as China's evidence discovery and disclosure. In fact, China's evidence presentation order is still young and needs further improvement, whereas the system of evidence discovery and disclosure has matured significantly in many countries. Therefore, we can only share our understanding of the difference between the two from a limited number of aspects.

First of all, in some countries, evidence discovery and disclosure can be divided into several stages. In the first stage, the discovery can be directly conducted by both parties out of court. Only at the disclosure stage, which requires the presentation of documents and physical evidence, does it involve requesting the court to compel the other party to disclose evidence. In China, all the procedures of the evidence presentation order need to be presided over by the court.

Secondly, the scope of application of China's evidence presentation order is limited to documentary evidence, audio-visual materials and electronic data, whereas the evidence discovery and disclosure may include any evidence related to the case.

Thirdly, China's evidence presentation order can only be made to the other party of the case. If it is necessary to collect evidence from the persons not involved in the case, the parties need to apply to the court for evidence investigation and collection or evidence preservation, the relevant rules of which are different from the evidence presentation order (for application to the court for evidence investigation and collection, see Sect. 6.11; for evidence preservation, see Sect. 6.13). In some countries, the evidence discovery and disclosure can be applied not only to the parties concerned but also those not involved in the case.

Finally, in some countries, refusing to disclose evidence as required by the court will not only lead to an unfavorable ruling, but will also result in such party's right to defend and present evidence being limited. However, China has no such provisions at present.

6.14.3 How to Apply to the Court for an Evidence Presentation Order

The parties shall submit an application to the court prior to the expiration of the time limit for presenting evidence. The application shall specify the following matters:

(1) The name or content of the evidence to be presented;
(2) What facts can be proved by the evidence and how important such facts are to the case; and
(3) The proof that the evidence is in the hands of the other party.

6.14.4 Application in Practice

We have carried out incomplete retrieval of judicial cases as of 2020 in China, including about 80 cases involving the evidence presentation order, in which IP-related cases outnumber others. A typical case is Shanghai Bacchus Wine Co., Ltd. v. Tonghua Dongte Wine Co., Ltd. [Case No.: (2017) Jing 73 Min Zhong No. 202, ((2017)京73民终202号)], one of the "Top Ten Intellectual Property Judicial Protection cases in Beijing courts" in 2017. In this case, the plaintiff requested the defendant to disclose relevant financial books to prove the profit obtained through the infringement, which was approved by the court, but the defendant did not submit the relevant evidence. Therefore, the court, combining other evidence presented by the plaintiff, ordered the defendant to make indemnification as per the upper limit of statutory indemnification.

There were also some cases where the courts dismissed the application, because the evidence required to be disclosed was not key evidence for the fact-finding. For example, in Sichuan ShuNiu Real Estate Development Co., Ltd. v. Ping An Bank Co., Ltd. Chengdu Branch [Case No.: (2017) Zui Gao Fa Min Shen No. 1400, ((2017) 最高法民申1400号)], the SPC held that ordering the disclosure of evidence by the other party shall simultaneously meet two conditions: the documentary evidence in question is of great significance to the facts to be proved, and the facts to be proved will impact the judgment. Given the documentary evidence in question failed to meet the above conditions, the application was therefore dismissed.

Generally speaking, the evidence presentation order in China's judicial practice still has a long way to go.

6.14.5 Prospect and Suggestions

As relevant judicial interpretations have already been revised recently, there may be no supplement and change to relevant rules of the evidence presentation order in the near future. Based on the dominant rule of "the burden of proof lies with/upon the party asserting a proposition" in China's civil litigation, in the foreseeable future, the parties should still focus on collecting evidence by themselves.

However, with the continuous improvement of Chinese laws, we believe that the evidence presentation order system will continue to develop and improve, and will be used more frequently. Even if the court dismisses such an application, the parties' litigious rights will not be affected (except, of course, for the punishment imposed due to the abuse of this system). Therefore, if the key evidence is controlled by the other party, we suggest that the party concerned try to make use of this system.

(Reference provisions and information for Sect. 6.14).[14]

---

[14] *Judicial Interpretation of CPL (Revised in 2022): Article 112, 113.*
Judicial Interpretation on Civil Evidence (Revised in 2019): Article 45, 99.

6.15 How to Keep Evidence Confidential in Litigation

In litigation, the party may encounter a dilemma: how to use the key evidence contains confidential information that is better not known by the other party. Is it possible to keep such information confidential in litigation and to what extent can such information be kept confidential? We will introduce some appropriate measures to protect the confidential information contained in the evidence.

In addition to the aforementioned methods, the parties can also request a non-public court trial or evidence examination, so as to prevent confidential evidence from being disclosed to the audience. If the court orders the parties to present unsubmitted evidence, the parties can also try some unconventional practices not stipulated by laws.

6.15.1 Try to Avoid Submitting Evidence Containing Confidential Information

In China, the parties may submit evidence selectively, but once the evidence is submitted, the copy of the evidence will be obtained by the other party and the judge. The judge will keep a copy in the case file for future inspection, presentation and examination in court by the parties. In addition, if the trial is held in public, it means that the evidence may be known by the audience (including online viewers). Therefore, the parties should be prudent when submitting evidence and try to avoid evidence with confidential information.

For the evidence involving confidential information, the parties may consider the following pros and cons at first:

(1) If the evidence in question is not submitted, will the probative force of other evidence be affected?
(2) To what extent can the parties tolerate the confidential information being known by others? And
(3) Which one matters more to the parties between the result of the case and the disclosure of the confidential information?

6.15.2 Cover Up the Confidential Part

For the confidential evidence that must be submitted, the parties may blacken the confidential part, such as the other party of the contract, the amount of transaction and sensitive terms etc., or extract non-confidential content only when preparing copies to the court. Of course, blackening and excerpt should be limited to a certain extent, which should neither affect the integrity of the whole document, nor cover up the content that plays a decisive role in judging the authenticity of the document (e.g., the formation time of the document, the official seal, the signature), so as to avoid unnecessary doubts about the authenticity of the evidence.

It should be noted that the original evidence needs to be presented to the other party in court for consistency check. Therefore, it is unrealistic to completely prevent the other party from accessing the confidential information contained in the evidence. However, the party concerned may request the judge to order the opposite party to sign a non-disclosure agreement, or even issue a ruling on this. In intellectual property-related cases, there are grounds for such practice in judicial interpretations of the SPC; meanwhile, some local courts have applied similar provisions to other cases. In addition, in some cases of trade secret infringement, the court will, upon the application of the parties, prohibit the other party from obtaining copies of the evidence, and only allow the evidence to be inspected and excerpted.

6.15.3 Request the Judge to Narrow Down the Scope of Evidence Presentation

In intellectual property and monopoly cases, if there is confidential information in the evidence, the parties may request the court to narrow down the scope of persons who can access the evidence. In trade secret cases, appraisal and examination is a very common procedure (for appraisal and examination, see Sect. 6.10), in which the expert opinions often need to quote the confidential information of both parties. In order to protect the confidential information, some courts have stipulated that the parties should only be informed of the conclusion without making available the specific materials to the parties; if the parties have any objection thereto, they can propose it to the court.

6.15.4 Request a Non-public Court Trial or Evidence Examination

In order to prevent confidential evidence from being disclosed to the audience, for the cases involving trade secrets and personal privacy (especially cases of trade secret infringement), the parties may apply for non-public trial or non-public examination, which will generally be supported by the court upon legal and justified reasons. In addition, the parties can also negotiate to recognize the evidence involving secrets at pre-trial conference, so as to avoid examination of the evidence during the court trial.

6.15.5 What if the Court Orders the Parties to Present Unsubmitted Evidence?

The court may investigate, collect, preserve or order the parties to submit evidence in their possession, thus resulting in the disclosure of confidential information in the following circumstances:

Firstly, the court carries out evidence preservation or orders the parties to submit evidence. Under specific circumstances, the court may take evidence preservation measures to directly search and detain the evidence not submitted by the party concerned (for evidence preservation, see Sect. 6.13). In addition, the court may, upon the application by the other party, order the parties to submit evidence (for evidence presentation order, see Sect. 6.14). The court may detain the original evidence in the aforesaid procedure, and the evidence so obtained shall be presented in court for examination.

Secondly, the other party applies for evidence authentication. If the other party applies for the evidence authentication and obtains the permission of the court, the party concerned needs to submit the original evidence to the court, which will transfer the same to the judicial expertise institution.

Undoubtedly, the above situations will undermine the parties' evidence confidentiality strategy. At this time, in order to maximize the protection of confidential information, in addition to the aforementioned methods, the parties can also try some unconventional practices. For example, the parties may request the judge to require the other party to provide corresponding guarantees by reference to the provisions of evidence preservation, so as to increase its litigation cost and procure its prudent exercise of such rights. Or, when verifying the consistency between the original and the copy of the evidence, the parties may try to request the judge to inform the other party of the verification result, instead of presenting the original directly to the other party. However, there is no clear legal basis for these practices, and the non-presentation of the original evidence to the other party is likely to incur strong objection. Therefore, the parties may give it a try if necessary, but should not rely too much on these practices.

(Reference provisions and information for Sect. 6.15).[15]

---

[15] *CPL (Revised in 2021): Article 137.*
Judicial Interpretation of CPL (Revised in 2022): Article 103.
Provisions of the Supreme People's Court on Evidence for Intellectual Property Civil Actions (Fa Shi [2020] No.12): Article 26.
《最高人民法院关于知识产权民事诉讼证据的若干规定》(法释〔2020〕12号).
Provisions of the Supreme People's Court on Several Issues Relating to the Application of Law in the Trial of Civil Dispute Cases Arising from Monopolies (Revised in 2020, Fa Shi [2012] No.5): Article 11.
《最高人民法院关于审理因垄断行为引发的民事纠纷案件应用法律若干问题的规定》(2020年修订, 法释〔2012〕5号).
Opinions of the Supreme People's Court on Several Issues Concerning Giving Full Play to the Intellectual Property Trial Function to Promote the Great Development and Prosperity of Socialist

Open Access This chapter is licensed under the terms of the Creative Commons Attribution 4.0 International License (http://creativecommons.org/licenses/by/4.0/), which permits use, sharing, adaptation, distribution and reproduction in any medium or format, as long as you give appropriate credit to the original author(s) and the source, provide a link to the Creative Commons license and indicate if changes were made.

The images or other third party material in this chapter are included in the chapter's Creative Commons license, unless indicated otherwise in a credit line to the material. If material is not included in the chapter's Creative Commons license and your intended use is not permitted by statutory regulation or exceeds the permitted use, you will need to obtain permission directly from the copyright holder.

Culture and Facilitate the Independent and Coordinated Development of Economy (Fa Fa [2011] No.18): Article 25.
《最高人民法院关于充分发挥知识产权审判职能作用推动社会主义文化大发展大繁荣和促进经济自主协调发展若干问题的意见》(法发〔2011〕18号).
Several Guiding Opinions of Henan Province High People's Court on the Trial of Trade Secret Infringement Disputes (For Trial Implementation): Article 10.
《河南省高级人民法院商业秘密侵权纠纷案件审理的若干指导意见(试行)》
Opinions of Jiangsu Province High People's Court on Issues Related to the Trial of Trade Secret Cases: Article 12.
《江苏省高级人民法院关于审理商业秘密案件有关问题的意见》

Chapter 7
Class Action in China?—Representative Litigation

Abstract In China, representative litigation is a system in which some members represent all members of the plaintiff in litigation, but the court judgment will be legally binding on all members being represented. There are similarities between China's representative litigation and the class action in some other countries. There were few representative litigation cases in China due to the lack of detailed legal provisions and other reasons. However, in 2020, China formulated more detailed legal provisions on the representative litigation system in the securities field. So far, China has established a set of complete and operable representative litigation rules for securities disputes. We expect to witness a gradual increase in the number of representative litigation cases in China, especially in the securities field.

7.1 What Is Representative Litigation

In China, representative litigation is a system in which some members of the plaintiff represent all members thereof (generally more than 10 in number) in a joint action. The litigation act of a representative shall have effect on all members he/she represents, but as to the change or waiver of the claim for relief, the admission of the claim for relief and reaching a settlement with the defendant, the representative must obtain the consent of the members being represented.

If the number of members of the plaintiff cannot be determined at the time of case filing, the court may issue an announcement to explain the circumstances of the case and the claims for relief, and notify other right holders to register with the court and join the representative litigation within a specified period of time. The time limit for announcement shall, while not less than 30 days, be subject to the specific circumstances of the case. The right holder applying for registration shall prove his legal relationship with the defendant and the damage he has suffered, otherwise the court may deny his application for registration.

For a long time, group action has been seldomly seen in China. The CPL (for Trial Implementation) promulgated in 1982 does not make special provisions on group action. In 1986, a group action occurred in Anyue County, Sichuan Province: 1569 rice seed operators sued Anyue County Seed Company, claiming that the seed company breached the rice seed production contract. At that time, the Primary People's Court of Anyue County adapted the joint action system then legally in force, adopted the practice that several farmers filed a lawsuit on behalf of hundreds of other farmers as the plaintiff, and then rendered a judgment legally binding on all farmers with similar sales contract disputes with the seed company. This case is a trail blazer in terms of group action in China.

In 1991, China promulgated the CPL, which gave birth to China's representative litigation system. The provisions of the latest version of the CPL (Revised in 2021) on representative litigation still remain consistent with those of the CPL effective in 1991. In addition, there are more detailed provisions on the representative litigation system in the relevant judicial interpretations of the CPL.

7.2 Who Will Be Bound by the Court Judgment in the Representative Litigation

For the representative litigation with a plaintiff consisting of a fixed number of members at the time of case filing, the court judgment will be binding on all members participating in the litigation.

For the representative litigation with a plaintiff consisting of uncertain number of members at the time of case filing, the court judgment will be binding on all registered members. For those right holders not registered, if they file a lawsuit within the limitation of action and the court considers that their claim for relief is tenable, then the judgment already in force will also be binding on them.

7.3 How to Determine the Representative

For the representative litigation with a plaintiff consisting of a fixed number of members at the time of case filing, the representatives are determined by the members themselves. The representatives may be jointly elected by all members, or each group of the members may elect their own representatives. Where the relevant groups fail to elect their own representatives, they may participate in the litigation themselves in case of a necessary joint action, or withdraw from the ongoing case and file a lawsuit separately in case of an ordinary joint action (for necessary joint action and ordinary joint action, see Sect. 6.4.3.4).

For the representative litigation with a plaintiff consisting of uncertain number of members at the time of case filing, the representatives shall be preferably elected by the registered members; if no representative is elected, the court may determine the representative through consultation with the registered members; If the consultation fails, the court may appoint a representative among the registered.

Regardless of the method adopted to determine the representatives, the number of representatives shall range from two to five. Like the parties in ordinary cases, each representative may entrust one or two persons as his agent ad litem.

7.4 China's Representative Litigation in Practice

Although the representative litigation system was established as early as 1991, the provisions of Chinese law on this system are too simple with many fields still left to be ploughed. The number of representative litigation cases in China has been remaining very small for a long time.

In June 2011, an oil spill accident occurred in the Penglai 19-3 oilfield of ConocoPhillips in the Bohai Sea. Many farmers near the polluted sea area filed a lawsuit against ConocoPhillips and requested ConocoPhillips to compensate for the losses incurred thereby. Viewed from the facts of the case, though the application conditions of representative litigation were met, the case was finally tried on a case-by-case basis according to the filing of each farmer.

However, in 2019, China revised its Securities Law and made new provisions on the representative litigation in the securities field. Accordingly, in 2020, the SPC formulated a more specific judicial interpretation for the representative litigation of securities disputes. In this context, the number of representative litigation cases in China began to increase rapidly. For example, the Shanghai Financial Court accepted China's first representative litigation case in the securities field: the case of Feilo Acoustics; the Beijing Financial Court accepted the securities representative litigation case concerning LETV; the Guangzhou Intermediate People's Court accepted the securities representative litigation case concerning Kangmei Pharmaceutical.

For more details about the representative litigation system in the securities field, please see following sections. We believe that the representative litigation system will play an increasingly important role in the protection of investors' rights and interests and other cases involving group interests.

(Reference provisions and information for Sects. 7.1–7.4).[1]

7.5 Representative Litigation for Securities Disputes

In 2019, China revised its Securities Law, clearly stipulating that the representative litigation system can be adopted for the securities civil compensation litigation and the dedicated investor protection institution may act as the representative of the plaintiff. In 2020, the SPC formulated a more specific judicial interpretation for the representative litigation of securities disputes.

---

[1] *CPL (Revised in 2021):* Article 53, 54.
Judicial Interpretation of CPL (Revised in 2022): Article 75–80.

Representative securities litigation can be categorized into two kinds: ordinary and special. In terms of the ordinary representative securities litigation, the representatives are preferably selected by investors and then appointed by the court. In terms of the special representative securities litigation, the investor protection institution will act as the representative of all investors by default, and investors who disagree with this arrangement need to make an explicit statement to withdraw from the litigation. By default, the representative enjoys many special rights to dispose of the rights and interests of investors. However, the representative will be subject to supervision and examination of the court when exercising these rights. We are looking forward to China promoting the representative litigation to more fields in the future.

7.5.1 The Newly Revised Securities Law Introduces the Representative Litigation System for Securities Dispute Resolution

On 28 December 2019, China promulgated its revised Securities Law, with an aim, among others, to strengthen the protection of investors. According to Article 95 of the revised Securities Law, the representative litigation system can be applied when investors file civil securities compensation litigation on such grounds as false statements. This is seen by many as a signal that China is ready to widely promote the representative litigation in the securities field.

More importantly, Article 95 of the Securities Law also creatively stipulates that if entrusted by more than 50 investors, China's investor protection institutions can participate in the litigation as representatives. In a litigation in which an investor protection institution is the representative, the investor protection institution may register with the court to participate in the litigation on behalf of all investors (subject to the list confirmed by the securities registration and settlement institution) of a security. If investors are unwilling to participate in the litigation, they need to make an explicit statement, i.e., investors "participate in by default but withdraw from such litigation by explicit statement".

The above litigation in which the investor protection institution participates as the representative is referred to as the special representative litigation. According to the regulations of China Securities Regulatory Commission, there are currently two investor protection institutions in China: one is China Securities Investor Service Center (中证中小投资者服务中心有限责任公司) based in Shanghai, and the other is China Securities Investor Protection Fund Corporation Limited (中国证券投资者保护基金有限责任公司) based in Beijing. Although these two organizations are for-profit legal persons, they are highly public interest-oriented when performing their duties of protecting the rights and interests of investors.

The ordinary representative litigation, a concept correlating with the special representative litigation, refers to the litigation in which the investor protection institution

7.5 Representative Litigation for Securities Disputes

does not act as the representative. The representative of such litigation shall still be selected from the members of the plaintiff in accordance with the CPL.

Although the Securities Law introduces the representative litigation system, the relevant provisions are too generalized, while the provisions of the CPL and its judicial interpretation on representative litigation are not detailed enough either. In order to translate the brief provisions into operable rules, the SPC promulgated the Provisions of the Supreme People's Court on Several Issues concerning Representative Litigation in Securities Disputes (最高人民法院关于证券纠纷代表人诉讼若干问题的规定) on 30 July 2020. So far, China has established a set of complete and operable representative litigation rules for securities disputes.

7.5.2 Basic Procedures for Starting the Representative Litigation for Securities Disputes

The basic procedures for starting the representative litigation for securities disputes include three steps:

(1) Investors file a lawsuit according to laws;
(2) Determine the scope of the plaintiff; and
(3) Determine the representative(s).

For the representative litigation in which the number of the members of the plaintiff is certain at the time of case filing, the scope and representative(s) of the plaintiff are usually certain as well at the time of case filing. For the representative litigation in which the number of the members of the plaintiff remain uncertain at the time of case filing, the procedures for its starting are more complex. Therefore, we will mainly introduce the starting procedures of this type of litigation.

7.5.3 Special Requirements for Starting Representative Litigation for Securities Disputes

To start the representative litigation for securities disputes, the plaintiff shall, in the statement of claim, propose 2–5 candidates as its proposed representatives at the time of case filing, and state the qualifications of such representatives in performing their duties.

More importantly, the plaintiff should also submit prima facie evidence to prove the securities infringement, such as administrative punishment decisions for securities law violations, criminal judgments, documents on disciplinary measures or self-discipline management measures taken by the stock exchange against the defendant, and announcements or statements of the defendant's self-admission on violations. Otherwise, the Chinese courts will not apply the representative litigation system for case hearing. This condition is set, on the one hand, to prevent the representative litigation system from being abused, and on the other hand, to prevent the process from stalling due to the lack of basic evidence, which will affect the trial efficiency and the interests of many investors.

7.5.4 How to Determine the Scope of the Plaintiff

If, after the plaintiff brings a lawsuit, the court considers that the number of members of the plaintiff cannot be determined, it shall first examine the nature and facts of the alleged securities infringement by means of files inspection and/or hearing. The time limit for examination is 30 days. The court shall, after the examination, make a ruling to determine the scope of right holders with the same claims for relief.

The court shall, within 5 days after making the above ruling, issue an announcement on right registration, notifying the right holders willing to file a lawsuit to register with the court within the specified time. The announcement period is 30 days.

The court shall, upon expiration of the registration period, complete the examination of the registered right holders within 10 days and include those qualified into the list of the plaintiff, which will then be issued by the court to all members of the plaintiff.

If any right holder fails to register with the court within the time specified by the announcement, he may apply to the court for supplementary registration before the first-instance court hearing. The litigation procedures completed before supplementary registration shall be binding on the said right holder.

7.5.5 How to Determine the Representative in Securities Disputes

7.5.5.1 Ordinary Representatives

In the ordinary representative litigation, the representative shall meet the following conditions:

(1) The representative acts as a representative voluntarily;
(2) The representative holds a certain proportion of interest in the litigation;
(3) The representative or his agent ad litem is capable of responding to litigation and has relevant experience;
(4) The representative is able to faithfully and diligently perform the duty of safeguarding the interests of all members of the plaintiff; and

7.5 Representative Litigation for Securities Disputes

(5) The representative is not affiliated with the defendant or falls under other circumstances that may affect his duty performance.

The ordinary representative shall be determined according to the following procedures:

Firstly, when filing a lawsuit, the plaintiff shall, in the statement of claim, propose 2–5 candidates as its proposed representatives, and state the qualifications of such representatives in performing their duties. If other investors neither raise any objection during the registration of rights announced by the court nor apply for acting as a representative, the court may appoint the candidates proposed in the statement of claim as the representatives.

Secondly, if there are no representatives proposed in the statement of claim, the court shall organize an election by voting among members of the plaintiff who voluntarily choose to act as representatives within 10 days upon determination of the scope of the plaintiff. "One Person, One Vote" shall be adopted in the election, and the number of votes obtained by each representative shall not be less than 50% of the number of voters. Since 2–5 representatives are required, if 2 or more representatives are elected through the first vote, the election will be completed. If less than 2 representatives are elected in Round 1 election, the court shall immediately organize the plaintiff to conduct a Round 2 election among the top five candidates.

Thirdly, if the two elections fail to produce qualified representatives, the court shall designate the representatives with the consent of the designated representatives.

7.5.5.2 Special Representatives

If, during the validity period of the registration announcement issued by the court, an investor protection institution as entrusted by more than 50 investors, decides to participate in the litigation, the investor protection institution will automatically become the representative. If more than two investor protection institutions meet the requirements, they shall determine the representative institution through negotiation. If the negotiation fails, the court shall appoint one of them as the representative. At this point, the special representative litigation is started.

Upon starting of the special representative litigation, if a member of the plaintiff who has filed the lawsuit does not want to participate in the special representative litigation, he may submit a withdrawal statement to the court. For such a member, the original litigation shall proceed. As for the type of procedures (such as ordinary representative litigation, joint action, or litigation based on the filing of each individual investor) with which the original litigation shall proceed, it should be determined according to the number of remaining investors and other factors. Besides, the court should also announce the basic information, litigation rights and the like of investor protection institutions to investors. According to the rule "participate in by default but withdraw from such litigation by explicit statement", if any investor does not agree to participate in the special representative litigation, he shall make a statement to the court within 15 days upon expiration of the announcement period, otherwise it shall be deemed to have agreed to participate in the litigation.

7.5.6 What Special Rights Does the Representative Enjoy in Securities Disputes

According to the CPL, the representative can change or waive the claim for relief, admit the claim of or reach a settlement agreement with the defendant only with the consent of the parties being represented.

However, in securities disputes, as long as an investor registers his right with the court, it is deemed that the investor grants the above litigation rights to the representative (be it an ordinary representative or an investor protection institution). In addition, the representative also has the right to, among others, file or waive an appeal, apply for the enforcement of effective judgments, and entrust agents ad litem.

It should be noted that although the representative enjoys the above-mentioned special authorizations, the exercise of these rights is subject to the supervision and examination of the court. For example, if the representative reaches a settlement agreement with the defendant, he needs to provide the settlement agreement and related matters to the court for examination. After examination by the court, the representative shall then notify the investors being represented to put forward opinions, and hold a hearing if the investors raise objections. Finally, the court shall decide whether to approve the settlement agreement. If the representative is prepared to change or waive some claims for relief (or even withdraw the lawsuit), or is going to admit the claim for relief of the defendant, he shall submit a written application to the court and notify all investors being represented of the same. The court shall have the final say to the application of the representative considering the objections raised by the investors.

Notwithstanding the foregoing, the investors being represented still have a say in terms of the foregoing rights. For example, if the court decides to approve the settlement agreement, the investor who once raised an objection may apply to withdraw from the mediation within 10 days after receiving the notice from the court; as to the representative's decision on appeal, the investor may either accept or deny the same at his sole discretion.

7.5.7 Practice and Future Prospects

On 18 August 2020, the Shanghai Financial Court accepted a lawsuit jointly filed by 34 plaintiffs including Wei Feng (魏锋) against Shanghai Feilo Acoustics Co., Ltd. for the securities dispute arising from false statements. This is also the first securities representative litigation accepted by a Chinese court under the new judicial interpretation.

In fact, there is great development potential for the representative litigation in many other fields such as product quality and environmental pollution. In the future, China may, based on the representative litigation rules in the securities field, further promote the representative litigation to other fields with an aim of more efficient dispute resolution.

(Reference provisions and information for Sect. 7.5).[2]

Open Access This chapter is licensed under the terms of the Creative Commons Attribution 4.0 International License (http://creativecommons.org/licenses/by/4.0/), which permits use, sharing, adaptation, distribution and reproduction in any medium or format, as long as you give appropriate credit to the original author(s) and the source, provide a link to the Creative Commons license and indicate if changes were made.

The images or other third party material in this chapter are included in the chapter's Creative Commons license, unless indicated otherwise in a credit line to the material. If material is not included in the chapter's Creative Commons license and your intended use is not permitted by statutory regulation or exceeds the permitted use, you will need to obtain permission directly from the copyright holder.

---

[2] *Securities Law of the People's Republic of China (Revised in 2019): Article 95.*
 Provisions of the Supreme People's Court on Several Issues regarding Representative Litigation in Securities Disputes (Fa Shi [2020] No.5): Article 1, 5–9, 11–16, 18–22, 27, 28, 32–34.
《最高人民法院关于证券纠纷代表人诉讼若干问题的规定》(法释〔2020〕5号)

Chapter 8
Civil Public Interest Litigation

Abstract In order to prevent and contain environmental pollution, protect consumers' rights and interests and other public interests, China is now establishing a public interest litigation system step by step. Compared with the private interest litigation, the public interest to be protected by the public interest litigation is an aggregation of private interests. However, the public interest litigation does not exclude the private interest litigation. While the public interest litigation is going on, the parties concerned may also file a private interest litigation and take a "free ride" in such aspects as evidence on the public interest litigation. In China, it is mainly the various types of social organizations registered with the civil affairs department that have the right to initiate a public interest litigation. Besides, the procuratorates may also initiate a civil public interest litigation in addition to their function of initiating a public prosecution against a crime. Compared with the private interest litigation, the public interest litigation has some special features in terms of the litigation procedures. In addition, the Chinese law also requires the court to intervene in the litigation with a more proactive manner and give certain help and tips to the plaintiff if necessary, with an aim to maximize the protection of public interests.

8.1 What Is Civil Public Interest Litigation

With China's rapid economic development and social transformation, environmental pollution, infringement on consumers' rights and interests and infringement on other public interests occur from time to time. In practice, the measures to curb these phenomena are, on the one hand, resorting to administrative punishment, i.e., the law enforcement by administrative authorities, and on the other hand, imposing criminal responsibility, i.e., if the act constitutes a crime, the offender will be held criminally responsible. However, neither administrative nor criminal measures can hold the tortfeasor civilly liable, such as claiming damages against the tortfeasor.

In order to solve this problem, the Supreme People's Procuratorate, as early as 1999, has required local procuratorates to try to bring a lawsuit against civil-law violations that infringe on national and/or public interests. However, China has not yet formulated any law on the public interest litigation, though there have been some public interest litigation cases in practice.

In 2012, China revised the CPL to stipulate that authorities and relevant organizations stipulated by the law may bring a lawsuit with the court against environmental pollution, infringement on consumers' rights and interests and other acts against the public interest. Although there is only one provision in the CPL, it marks China's official establishment of the civil public interest litigation system. Since then, the SPC has successively formulated several special judicial interpretations for the civil public interest litigation on environmental pollution and infringement on consumers' rights and interests.

So far, China has initially established a civil public interest litigation system. Compared with the private interest litigation, the public interest to be protected by the public interest litigation is an aggregation of private interests; however, the aggregated private interests, though composed of specific individual interests, are relatively abstract and generalized, and it is often difficult to identify the specific right holder. Besides, the wrongful act targeted by the public interest litigation tends to be generalized and covert. Therefore, ordinary natural persons or enterprises often lack the ability and motivation to file a suit, and this is exactly why China establishes the public interest litigation system.

8.2 Public Interest Litigation Versus Private Interest Litigation

In China, the ongoing public interest litigation does not affect the infringed to file a private interest litigation according to law. On the contrary, the public interest litigation may also contribute to the private interest litigation in the following aspects.

Firstly, as for the facts found by the effective judgment of a public interest litigation, neither the plaintiff nor the defendant of the private interest litigation needs to present evidence for such facts again. Unless either party presents evidence to the contrary to overturn such findings (only the plaintiff may do so in environmental protection litigation), the facts found by the effective judgment of a public interest litigation shall prevail. In terms of the legal nature of the defendant's act, the cause and effect between the defendant's act and the environmental pollution, and the legal liability of the defendant, if the findings of a public interest litigation are favorable to the plaintiff, the plaintiff can claim that such findings be directly applied, while the defendant needs to present evidence to the contrary to overturn such findings. However, if the findings of a public interest litigation are favorable to the defendant, the defendant cannot claim that such findings be directly applied, but shall present further evidence to support his claim. In other words, the plaintiff of the private interest litigation may take a "free ride" on the findings of the public interest litigation, which actually reduces his burden of proof in the private interest litigation.

Secondly, in the private interest litigation filed by consumers, if the corresponding public interest litigation has been lodged, consumers can apply for suspension of the private interest litigation and wait for the judgment of the public interest litigation, so as to make full use of the "free rider" right.

Thirdly, in the environmental protection litigation, if the defendant is held liable in both public and private interest litigation, while his property is insufficient to cover all liabilities, then he should first perform the obligations under the judgment of the private interest litigation. This has reflected the special care for private rights and interests provided by the Chinese law.

8.3 Who May File a Civil Public Interest Litigation

At present, in China, there are mainly two types of subjects that may file a civil public interest litigation: social organizations and procuratorates.

8.3.1 Social Organizations

The term "social organizations" mainly refers to social organizations, foundations and social service agencies, etc. registered with the civil affairs department. For example, All-China Environmental Federation (中华环保联合会), China Biodiversity Conservation and Green Development Foundation (中国生物多样性保护与绿色发展基金会) and Beijing Friends of Nature Public Welfare Foundation (北京自然之友公益基金会) are well-known social organizations in the field of environmental protection; China Consumers Association (中国消费者协会) and various local consumers associations are well-known social organizations in the field of consumers' rights and interests protection.

Generally speaking, the purpose and business scope of a social organization that files a public interest litigation should be related to the public interest involved in the litigation. Therefore, social organizations generally cannot file a public interest litigation against infringement outside their own fields. The public interest litigation related to consumers' rights and interests is generally initiated by China Consumers Association and various local consumers associations. Pursuant to the Chinese law, to be qualified to file an environmental public interest litigation, a social organization shall meet the following conditions:

(1) Registers with the civil affairs department of the government at or above the districted city level according to law;
(2) The purpose and main business scope defined in its articles of association include safeguarding social and public interests;
(3) Engages in environmental protection public welfare activities for more than five consecutive years; and

(4) Has not been subject to administrative and/or criminal punishment due to violation of laws and/or regulations during the five years prior to the public interest litigation.

There has been no explicit provision in the Chinese law yet with respect to which social organizations should file other types of public interest litigation. However, we believe that such circumstances may be handled with reference to the relevant provisions on the environmental public interest litigation.

8.3.2 Procuratorates

The main duty of China's procuratorates is to initiate public prosecution against crimes (also including investigation of job-related crimes in the past). Besides, the procuratorate also assumes the duty to supervise civil and administrative cases by lodging a protest. China, after a series of reform and experimental measures, revised the Organic Law of the People's Procuratorates of the People's Republic of China in 2018 to include the filing of public interest litigation into the duties of the procuratorates.

According to the Chinese law, there are two ways for a procuratorate to initiate a public interest litigation:

First, the procuratorate shall make an announcement for a period of 30 days in accordance with the law upon discovering an infringement on the public interest. Upon expiration of the announcement period, only if the authority or social organization that has the right to file a public interest litigation fails to do so, may the procuratorate file a public interest litigation instead; if the said authority or social organization files a public interest litigation, then the procuratorate can provide support to the authority or social organization by providing advice and/or assisting in investigation and evidence collection.

Second, the procuratorate may, while filing a criminal public prosecution against a crime that damages the public interest, bring an incidental civil public interest litigation with the court.

Furthermore, the Chinese law classifies acts that infringe upon the name, portrait, reputation and honor of heroes and martyrs as acts that infringe upon the public interest. Given the particularity of this type of cases, we won't walk you through this issue for the time being.

In the public interest litigation filed by the procuratorate, the procuratorate is not called the "plaintiff", but rather the "public interest litigation prosecutor". The procuratorate shall enjoy the litigation rights stipulated in the CPL as well, unless otherwise provided by the law.

8.4 Announcement Is Required for a Public Interest Litigation

With respect to the environmental public interest litigation and the public interest litigation related to consumers' rights and interests protection, the court shall, after accepting the case, announce the acceptance thereof to the public at large, so as to ensure the public's right to know. Other social organizations that have the right to file a public interest litigation may also apply to join the litigation as a co-plaintiff within 30 days as of the announcement date.

If the public interest litigation is initiated by the procuratorate, given the procuratorate has made an announcement before prosecution, the court does not need to make an announcement again after accepting the case.

8.5 The Competent Administrative Department Shall Be Informed of the Public Interest Litigation

The court shall, in addition to making an announcement to the public, notify the relevant competent administrative departments in writing within 10 days after accepting the environmental public interest litigation and the public interest litigation related to consumers' rights and interests protection, with an aim to urge the administrative authorities to take law enforcement actions in a timely manner and curb the infringement as soon as possible while initiating the civil proceedings.

Generally speaking, for an environmental public interest litigation, the court shall inform the local environmental protection bureau; for a public interest litigation related to consumers' rights and interests, the court shall inform the local market regulation authority.

8.6 The Court May Intervene in the Legal Proceedings with a More Proactive Manner

As it involves public interests, Chinese law requires the court to be more proactive in public interest litigation to maximize the intended effect of such litigation. Compared with the private interest litigation, there are some specific examples of court intervention in the public interest litigation proceedings:

Firstly, in most cases of private interest litigation, Chinese courts will not take the initiative to investigate and collect evidence. However, in cases of public interest litigation, the court may take the initiative to investigate and collect evidence (for investigation and collection of evidence by the court, see Sect. 6.11). Especially in the environmental civil public interest litigation, the judicial interpretation of the SPC specifically emphasizes that the court should investigate and collect the evidence as it deems necessary, and may arrange an appraisal or examination on the specialized issues for which the plaintiff should bear the burden of proof (for appraisal and examination and expert opinions, see Sect. 6.10).

Secondly, in the private interest litigation, the defendant needs not to bear the burden of proof for the facts and evidence unfavorable to and admitted by the plaintiff, and the court can directly find the facts of the case based on the self-admission (for self-admission system, see Sect. 6.4). However, in the public interest litigation, if the facts admitted by the plaintiff (including the procuratorate as the "public interest litigation prosecutor") damage the public interest, the court shall not endorse such facts.

Thirdly, in the private interest litigation, Chinese courts generally follow the principle of "No Trial Without Complaint" and will not inform the plaintiff of the type of claims he should make. However, in the public interest litigation, if the court considers that the claim made by the plaintiff is insufficient to protect the public interest, it may prompt the plaintiff to change the claim or make more claims.

Fourthly, in the environmental public interest litigation, if the parties reach a settlement, the court shall announce the settlement agreement so reached to the public for a period of not less than 30 days. The court may, upon expiration of the announcement period, render a settlement statement only if it considers that the settlement agreement so reached does not damage the social and public interests. Besides, the settlement statement shall be made public. In contrast, the mediation in the private interest litigation is generally conducted privately and the mediation statement will not be made public as well.

(Reference provisions and information for this Chapter)[1]

---

[1] *CPL (Revised in 2021): Article 58.*

Environmental Protection Law of the People's Republic of China (Revised in 2014): Article 58.
《中华人民共和国环境保护法》(2014年修订).

Interpretation of the Supreme People's Court on Several Issues Concerning the Application of Law in the Hearing of Environment-related Civil Public Interest Lawsuits (Revised in 2020, Fa Shi [2015] No.1): Article 2, 4, 5, 9–12, 14, 16, 25, 29–31.
《最高人民法院关于审理环境民事公益诉讼案件适用法律若干问题的解释》(2020年修订, 法释〔2015〕1号).

Interpretation of the Supreme People's Court on Several Issues Concerning the Application of Law in the Hearing of Environment-related Civil Public Interest Lawsuits (Revised in 2020, Fa Shi [2016] No.10): Article 1, 5–7, 9, 10, 12, 16.
《最高人民法院关于审理消费民事公益诉讼案件适用法律若干问题的解释》(2020年修订, 法释〔2016〕10号).

Interpretation of the Supreme People's Court and the Supreme People's Procuratorate on Several Issues Concerning the Application of Law in the Hearing of Procuratorate-related Civil Public Interest Lawsuits (Revised in 2020): Article 4, 13, 17, 18, 20.
《最高人民法院、最高人民检察院关于检察公益诉讼案件适用法律若干问题的解释》(2020年修订).

Open Access This chapter is licensed under the terms of the Creative Commons Attribution 4.0 International License (http://creativecommons.org/licenses/by/4.0/), which permits use, sharing, adaptation, distribution and reproduction in any medium or format, as long as you give appropriate credit to the original author(s) and the source, provide a link to the Creative Commons license and indicate if changes were made.

The images or other third party material in this chapter are included in the chapter's Creative Commons license, unless indicated otherwise in a credit line to the material. If material is not included in the chapter's Creative Commons license and your intended use is not permitted by statutory regulation or exceeds the permitted use, you will need to obtain permission directly from the copyright holder.

Chapter 9
Property Preservation and Act Preservation

Abstract In China, some defendants will, upon becoming aware of being sued, take various methods to transfer and/or hide their property or the subject matter in dispute. In such circumstances, even if the plaintiff wins the case, it may still find it difficult to be actually compensated. In order to solve this problem, the plaintiff can apply to the Chinese court for property preservation. Chinese courts will take such preservation measures as sequestering, seizing and/or freezing according to the type of property to be preserved, which are the same as those taken by the courts during the enforcement procedure. In order to avoid "winning the case but still losing money", it'd be better for the plaintiff to consider applying for property preservation and collect property clues of the defendant before case filing. Act preservation is a temporary remedy to avoid the parties from suffering "irreparable damage" during the civil proceedings. The act preservation is highly similar to the "interlocutory injunction" in common law countries and the "provisional injunction" in civil law countries such as Germany and Japan. Chinese courts, when examining the application for act preservation, need to balance the interests between the parties and the public. In recent years, the number of cases, especially those related to intellectual property and unfair competition, subject to the act preservation measures has been on the rise. If the application for act preservation is erroneous, the applicant shall be liable for compensation to the respondent. In intellectual property and unfair competition cases, there are clear-cut standards for determining whether an application for act preservation is erroneous or not.

9.1 Property Preservation—The Key to Prevent Defendants from Transferring/Hiding Property

9.1.1 What Is Property Preservation

Property preservation is a compulsory measure taken by the court to sequester, seize and/or freeze the property of the respondent or the subject matter in dispute, with an aim to prevent the respondent from transferring and/or concealing property or the subject matter in dispute, and to ensure the enforcement of a later effective judgment.

Generally speaking, the property preservation will only be initiated upon application by the plaintiff with the court. Although the court may also take the initiative to impose the preservation measures if it deems it necessary, in practice, the property preservation is still initiated upon application by the plaintiff under most circumstances.

When examining the application for property preservation, the most important factor to be considered by the court is: whether there are circumstances, e.g., an act that the respondent has performed or may perform, that will make it difficult to enforce the later effective judgment or cause the applicant to suffer other damages. However, this standard is quite ambiguous and the judge needs to make a judgment on a case-by-case basis. Based on this, Chinese courts, on the one hand, are not that inclined to take the property preservation against institutions with good credit status such as banks and listed companies, but on the other hand, are more willing to take the property preservation against institutions with general credit status and natural persons.

In addition, for arbitration cases conducted in Mainland China, the claimant may also submit an application for property preservation with the court through the arbitration institution.

9.1.2 How to Apply for the Property Preservation?

The plaintiff needs to submit an application for property preservation to the court and provide the court with property clues of the respondent as detailed as possible. Generally, such property clues include:

(1) Bank account information (bank name, account number, account name, etc.);
(2) Real estate information (location of the land, accurate address of a building, etc.);
(3) Vehicle information (vehicle model, license plate number, etc.); and
(4) Shareholding information (company name, registered capital of the company, shareholding ratio and corresponding capital contribution, etc.).

The plaintiff can, in addition to providing property clues, request the court to use the Online Enforcement Query and Control System (for the Online Enforcement Query and Control System and the enforcement, see Sect. 10.3) to investigate the respondent's property as well. However, in practice, a considerable number of courts believe that the Online Enforcement Query and Control System cannot be used to help the plaintiff track down the respondent's property for the purpose of property preservation. Therefore, providing accurate and detailed property clues is particularly important for the successful implementation of property preservation. In respect of real estate, vehicles and other properties subject to registration, it would be better if the plaintiff could provide a copy of the registration certificate.

The application for property preservation may be submitted to the court at the time of case filing or after the case docketing. If an application for property preservation is submitted at the time of case filing, many Chinese courts will first examine the application for property preservation and take preservation measures (if they agree to implement the preservation measures), and then deliver the relevant court documents to the respondent, so as to prevent the respondent from transferring and/or hiding property after becoming aware of being sued. If the failure to apply for preservation immediately under urgency will cause irreparable damage to the legitimate rights and interests of the parties (e.g., there is evidence that the respondent is transferring its main property), the plaintiff may also apply for property preservation before case filing. However, the plaintiff shall submit evidence proving the urgency and explain the possible consequences arising from not taking preservation measures. If the court agrees to take the property preservation, the parties shall file a case within 30 days thereafter. However, in practice, it is quite difficult to apply for pre-litigation property preservation.

9.1.3 How Chinese Courts Implement the Property Preservation

Chinese courts will adopt different property preservation measures according to the specific types of property to be preserved. The specific measures are the same as those taken by the court during the enforcement procedure (for the enforcement procedure, see Chap. 10). We will take the following commonly seen properties as examples:

(1) For bank deposits, the court will generally order the bank to freeze the bank account of the respondent;
(2) For real estate, vehicles, ships, equity and other properties subject to registration, the court will generally order the registration authority not to handle the ownership transfer and mortgage registration for the property to be preserved; and
(3) For movable property not subject to registration, the court may seize the property, or not seize the property while affixing a seal to the property or ordering the respondent not to dispose of or damage the property.

The court may, if necessary, also impose multiple property preservation measures on one piece of property to be preserved, for example, the court may order the registration authority to cease handling the ownership transfer registration for a building, and affix a seal to the building at the same time to prohibit others from entering and using the building. However, it should be noted that, according to the requirements of the SPC, the court should, without prejudice to the preservation effect, try to take preservation measures that do not affect the respondent's use of property as far as possible, with an aim to reduce the unnecessary impact on the respondent, and to allow the respondent to use the preserved property for further business activities, so that the respondent may have a better chance to repay its debt.

It is worth mentioning that in the past, judges needed to go to banks, property registration authorities or other places personally to verify the information of the property to be preserved before implementing the property preservation. However, after the establishment of the Online Enforcement Query and Control System, the court can complete the foregoing steps online, greatly improving the efficiency of property preservation. Most banks in China have now connected to the Online Enforcement Query and Control System, while the property registration authorities still vary from one to another in terms of connecting to the said system. There is no doubt that, with the gradual improvement of the said system, the efficiency of property preservation by Chinese courts will rise with the tide as well.

9.1.4 The Validity Period of Property Preservation

The validity period of property preservation depends on the type of property to be preserved:
(1) For bank deposits, the validity period can be up to one year;
(2) For movables (including vehicles, ships and other movables subject to registration), the validity period can be up to two years; and
(3) For real estate, equity and other property rights, the validity period can be up to three years.

However, the parties may, prior to the expiration of the validity period of property preservation, apply for a renewal thereof for several times until the court renders an effective judgment and completes the enforcement procedure.

9.1.5 The Consequences of Violating a Court Order

If a respondent, in violation of the property preservation order of the court, conceals, transfers, sells off or damages the property to be preserved, then the court may impose a fine on the respondent, detain the respondent, or even hold the respondent criminally responsible. If the respondent is a natural person, the amount of fine shall be less than RMB 100,000, and the period of detention shall be less than 15 days; if the respondent commits a crime, he can also be sentenced to fixed-term imprisonment of less than 3 years. If the respondent is an organization, the amount of fine will range from RMB 50,000 to RMB 1,000,000; the principal or directly responsible person of the organization can also be held liable according to the above standards.

If the bank, property registration authority and other organizations refuse to assist in the property preservation as per the court order, the court may impose a fine on the organization and/or its principal or directly responsible person, and/or detain principal or directly responsible person according to the above standards.

9.1.6 Application Fee Charged by the Court

The plaintiff, in addition to the normal court costs, also needs to pay to the court a preservation application fee up to RMB 5,000 according to the value of the property to be preserved.

9.1.7 Providing Guarantee and Relevant Fees

Given that the property preservation measures will restrict the respondent from disposing of and/or using the property, if the plaintiff wrongly or even maliciously applies for property preservation, the respondent may thereby suffer losses. Therefore, the court generally requires the plaintiff to provide a guarantee, the specific amount of which depends on the value of the property to be preserved and the specific circumstances of the case. For general property preservation, the guarantee amount shall not exceed 30% of the value of the property to be preserved or the subject matter in dispute. If pre-litigation property preservation is applied for, generally speaking, the amount of guarantee must be 100% of the value of the property to be preserved.

Generally speaking, the types of frequently adopted guarantee include:

(1) Cash/bank deposits;
(2) A physical objects, such as a commercial residential apartment under the name of the respondent or others, attached with the valuation report issued by an asset valuation agency if necessary;
(3) A letter of guarantee issued by an insurance company after the applicant signing a property preservation liability insurance contract with the insurance company; and
(4) An independent guarantee issued by banks and other financial institutions.

If the applicant provides a guarantee by such means as a physical object, a letter of guarantee from an insurance company, an independent guarantee from a financial institution, etc., he/she also need to pay a certain service fee, the specific amount of which is subject to the actual situation, to the valuation agency, insurance company and financial institution.

9.1.8 Our Advice

According to our experience, it is not uncommon for the defendant to transfer and/or conceal its property in China. In order to avoid "winning the case but still losing money", we advise that the plaintiff consider applying for property preservation and try to collect property clues before case filing. According to our experience, it is generally the best practice to submit an application for property preservation at the time of filing a statement of claim. This practice, on the one hand, avoids the court from applying the stringent examination standard of pre-litigation preservation application, thus reducing the burden of the plaintiff in terms of providing a guarantee, and on the other hand, maximizes the suddenness and intended effect of the preservation measures.

(Reference provisions and information for Sect. 9.1).[1]

9.2 Act Preservation—China's "Interlocutory Injunction"

9.2.1 What Is Act Preservation

Act preservation is a mandatory measure of the court to order a party to do or refrain from doing certain acts in order to avoid damage to the other party pending an effective judgment of the case. According to the contents of the request, the act preservation can be divided into act preservation (such as ordering the respondent to eliminate the nuisance) and omission preservation (such as ordering the respondent to refrain from doing certain acts).

There are similarities between the basic rules of act preservation and those of property preservation (for property preservation, see Sect. 9.1). For example, in most cases, the act preservation is initiated upon application by the parties, and generally, the application is made during the litigation, and in case of urgency, the application for act preservation can be made before case filing; the applicant shall specify the purpose, target and specific measures to be taken of the act preservation, and provide necessary evidence therefor; to apply for an act preservation, generally, a guarantee shall be provided and an application fee shall be paid to the court.

However, compared with the property preservation, the act preservation often has a greater impact on the parties concerned. The property preservation is only a temporary restriction on the respondent's disposal of property to ensure the enforcement of a later effective judgment, while the act preservation often requires the respondent to stop production, sales and other business activities immediately, producing basically the same effect as enforcing an effective judgment. In the cases of infringement of intellectual property rights and unfair competition (especially the cases of infringement committed through the Internet), the damage caused by the infringement to the right holder (especially the damage to goodwill and/or market share) is often irreversible, and the consequences arising therefrom are likely to expand in the wink

---

[1] *CPL (Revised in 2021): Article 103–106, 114.*
Judicial Interpretation of CPL (Revised in 2022): Article 156, 165, 168, 485.
Judicial Interpretation on Property Preservation (Revised in 2020).
Provisions of the Supreme People's Court on Sequestering, Seizing, and Freezing Property in Civil Enforcement by People's Courts (Revised in 2020).
《最高人民法院关于人民法院民事执行中查封、扣押、冻结财产的规定》(2020年修订).
Measures for the Payment of Litigation Fees: Article 14.
《诉讼费用交纳办法》.

9.2 Act Preservation—China's "Interlocutory Injunction"

of an eye. Therefore, even if the right holder wins the case, it may have lost its competitive advantage in the market, or its trade secret has been divulged. In that case, it is necessary to apply for act preservation and request the court to order the respondent to do or refrain from doing certain acts.

In fact, it was in the field of intellectual property rights where China established the act preservation system first. China introduced the act preservation system when revising the Copyright Law, the Trademark Law and the Patent Law during 2001 to 2002. In 2012, China revised the CPL to extend the act preservation to all civil-law fields, but intellectual property and unfair competition are still the fields where the act preservation is applied most frequently. In 2012, Guangzhou Pharmaceutical Holdings Limited (广州医药集团有限公司) applied with the court to order Guangdong JDB Beverage and Food Co., Ltd. (广东加多宝饮料食品有限公司) not to use such taglines as "Wong Lo Kat is now changed to JDB (王老吉改名为加多宝)", and the court supported the application; in 2013, Eli Lilly and Company, an American pharmaceutical company, successfully applied with the court for an injunction, ordering its former employee not to disclose, use or allow others to use 21 confidential documents obtained from the Company; in 2016, Zhejiang Tangde Film and Television Co., Ltd. (浙江唐德影视股份有限公司) applied with the court to order Shanghai Canxing Media Co., Ltd. (上海灿星文化传播有限公司), et al., to stop using "The Voice of China (中国好声音)" as the name of its TV programs, and the respondent was compelled to change its program name before going online. In recent years, most of the guiding cases of act preservation in Chinese courts also come from the intellectual property related field.

9.2.2 How Chinese Courts Examine the Application for Act Preservation

In December 2018, the SPC issued a judicial interpretation, specifically providing for the act preservation in intellectual property and unfair competition cases. According to the said judicial interpretation, Chinese courts will, when examining an application for act preservation, mainly consider the following four factors:

(1) Whether the applicant's request has a factual and legal basis, including whether the validity of the intellectual property right to be protected is stable;
(2) Whether the failure to adopt act preservation measures will cause irreparable damage to the legitimate rights and interests of the applicant or make it difficult to enforce the court judgement. In respect of intellectual property and unfair competition cases, "irreparable damage" includes: the respondent's act will infringe upon the applicant's personal rights such as goodwill or publication right and/or the right to privacy and cause irreparable damage thereto; it is difficult to control the infringement and the infringement will significantly increase the damage to the applicant; it will result in a significant reduction in the relevant market share of the applicant; and the like;

(3) Whether the damage caused to the applicant due to not adopting act preservation measures exceeds the damage caused to the respondent due to doing so; and
(4) Whether the adoption of act preservation measures will damage the public interest.

As the examination of the application for act preservation generally requires the investigation and review of the substantive issues of the case, the examination procedure of the court is generally more stringent compared with the property preservation. According to the foresaid judicial interpretation, the court shall inform the parties of the same before adopting the act preservation measures, unless the situation is urgent or the informing may affect the implementation thereof.

Although the above provisions are made for the act preservation in intellectual property and unfair competition cases, they are still of significant reference value for other cases. In practice, Chinese courts are very likely to examine the application for act preservation submitted by the parties of other types of cases with reference to the above provisions.

9.2.3 The Validity Period of Act Preservation

The validity period of act preservation shall be reasonably determined on a case-by-case basis and based on the preservation measures adopted. If the preservation measure is to stop infringement, the validity period thereof shall generally last until the judgment takes effect. The court may also, upon determination of the validity period of preservation, extend it considering the request of the applicant, the additional guarantee provided by the applicant, etc. In addition, generally, the act preservation measures will not be lifted only because the respondent provides a counter guarantee, unless otherwise agreed by the applicant.

9.2.4 The Consequences of Violating a Court Order

The consequences of violating an act preservation order are the same as those of violating a property preservation order, i.e., the court may impose a fine on the respondent, detain the respondent, or even hold the respondent criminally responsible.

9.2.5 The Consequences of an Erroneous Application for Act Preservation

If the applicant wrongly applies for an act preservation against the respondent, it shall be liable for compensation to the respondent, and the consequences are the same as those of wrongly applying for a property preservation. However, the definition of an erroneous application for property preservation is quite ambiguous, and Chinese courts tend to be very cautious in making relevant judgments as well. In contrast, in respect of intellectual property rights and unfair competition cases, there are clear-cut standards for determining whether an application for act preservation is erroneous or not:

(1) The applicant applies for pre-litigation act preservation under urgency and obtains the permission of the court, but fails to file a case or apply for arbitration within 30 days upon adoption of the preservation measures in accordance with the law;
(2) The act preservation measures are inappropriate ab initio due to the invalidation of the intellectual property right to be protected, etc.;
(3) The applicant applies for ordering the respondent to stop infringing intellectual property rights or unfair competition, but the later effective judgment finds that the respondent does not commit any infringement or unfair competition; and
(4) Other situations of erroneous application.

Therefore, we advise that the parties carefully evaluate whether the right to be protected is stable and the possibility of winning the case before applying for an act preservation, so as to avoid being held liable for compensation due to an erroneous application for act preservation.

(Reference provisions and information for Sect. 9.2)[2]

---

[2] *CPL (Revised in 2021): Article 100, 104.*
Judicial Interpretation of CPL (Revised in 2022): Article 152.
Provisions of the Supreme People's Court on Several Issues concerning the Application of Law in Reviewing the Injunction Cases involving Intellectual Property Disputes (Fa Shi [2018] No.21): Article 5–7, 10–13, 16.
《最高人民法院关于审查知识产权纠纷行为保全案件适用法律若干问题的规定》(法释〔2018〕21号).

Open Access This chapter is licensed under the terms of the Creative Commons Attribution 4.0 International License (http://creativecommons.org/licenses/by/4.0/), which permits use, sharing, adaptation, distribution and reproduction in any medium or format, as long as you give appropriate credit to the original author(s) and the source, provide a link to the Creative Commons license and indicate if changes were made.

The images or other third party material in this chapter are included in the chapter's Creative Commons license, unless indicated otherwise in a credit line to the material. If material is not included in the chapter's Creative Commons license and your intended use is not permitted by statutory regulation or exceeds the permitted use, you will need to obtain permission directly from the copyright holder.

Chapter 10
Enforcement

Abstract In China, if the losing party does not take the initiative to satisfy an effective court judgment, arbitral award and other legal documents, the winning party may apply to the court for enforcement. Then the court may deduct the deposit and/or auction the property of the losing party and use the money/proceeds obtained therefrom to repay the winning party. However, this enforcement power is exclusively vested in the court, and the winning party cannot seize and/or dispose of the property of the losing party on its own. Due to the large number of enforcement cases, the difficulty in tracking down enforceable property and the insufficient punishment against dishonest judgment debtors, China has been plagued by the "difficulty in enforcement" for a long time. In China, the main reason for the "difficulty in enforcement" is that it is difficult to track down the enforceable property of the party subject to enforcement. In order to resolve this problem, Chinese courts have vigorously promoted the information system interconnection between different government departments, which has greatly improved the efficiency of tracking down and/or freezing the property of the party subject to enforcement through the information network system. Another reason for the "difficulty in enforcement" is that it is difficult to sell off non-cash properties. Chinese courts have carried out judicial auctions through the Internet, which has greatly improved the deal closing rate and increased the transaction price of the property auctioned, and greatly improved the possibility of the applicant being compensated. Other than the above approaches, Chinese courts may also impose various restrictions and punishments on dishonest judgment debtors. There are various restrictions and punishments and the implementation thereof depends on the interconnection of different information network systems. If the circumstances in which the party subject to enforcement evades or resists enforcement are serious, the Chinese court may also hold it criminally responsible. In addition, being a contracting state to the United Nations Convention on the Recognition and Enforcement of Foreign Arbitral Awards (hereinafter referred to as the "New York Convention"), China has been holding a quite friendly attitude towards the recognition and enforcement of foreign arbitral awards. In practice, most foreign arbitral awards can be recognized and enforced in China. Compared with the recognition and enforcement of foreign arbitral awards, there are more requirements and preconditions for the recognition and enforcement of foreign court judgments. Nevertheless, China is now relaxing these requirements and preconditions, and more and more foreign court judgments are being recognized and enforced. With continuous efforts of relevant departments, the enforcement conducted by Chinese courts is getting increasingly effective. We firmly believe that Chinese courts can further improve the enforcement effectiveness as day goes by.

10.1 What Is Enforcement and Some Basic Points

The term "enforcement" refers to the act of the court to force the party subject to enforcement to perform the obligations under effective legal documents by means of the state coercion. In China, the enforcement power is exclusively vested in the court. Therefore, even if the losing party fails to take the initiative to satisfy an effective legal document, the winning party still cannot seize and/or dispose of the losing party's property on its own, and must apply to the court for enforcement. The court can take a variety of enforcement measures and the proceeds thus obtained will be used to repay the winning party. Generally, such enforcement measures include, inter alia, deducting the bank deposits of the party subject to enforcement, sequestering and auctioning other property of the party subject to enforcement.

The enforcement procedure can be applied to not only effective judgments made by courts, but also settlement statements made by courts, arbitral awards made by arbitration institutions, and notarized creditor's right documents prepared as per certain procedures. Besides, effective foreign court judgments and arbitral awards recognized by Chinese courts may be enforced in China as well (for recognition and enforcement of foreign arbitral awards and foreign court judgments, see Sects. 10.6 and 10.7).

Different types of legal documents are enforced by different courts. For example, the court judgment is generally enforced by the court of first instance or the court at the same level as the court of first instance of the place where the enforceable property is located; the arbitral award is generally enforced by the intermediate court of the place where the party subject to enforcement resides or where the enforceable property is located (for the 4-level Chinese courts system, see Sect. 1.1).

The time limit for applying for enforcement (referred to as the "limitation of application for enforcement" under the Chinese law) is two years upon expiration of the performance period specified in the effective legal document. In the future, the limitation of application for enforcement is very likely to be extended to three years, as long as the limitation of action. Like the limitation of action, the limitation of application for enforcement can be reset by the assertion of right by the right holder, or suspended under specific circumstances; the specific rules of the limitation of application for enforcement are the same as those of the limitation of action.

When applying for enforcement, the applicant need not pay the application fee. The application fee shall be deducted by the court from the property obtained from the enforcement. In practice, sometimes Chinese courts even do not charge application fees, which is undoubtedly favorable to the applicant. The progressive application rates for enforcement are as follows:

Enforcement amount (X)	Application fee
< RMB 10,000	RMB 50
RMB 10,000—RMB 500,000	1.5% X—RMB 100
RMB 500,000—RMB 5,000,000	1% X + RMB 2400
RMB 5,000,000—RMB 10,000,000	0.5% X + RMB 27,400
> RMB 10,000,000	0.1% X + RMB 67,400

(Reference provisions and information for Sect. 10.1).[1]

10.2 China Has Long Been Plagued by the "Difficulty in Enforcement"

Despite the guarantee of state coercion, many legal instruments are still remained to be enforced due to the following reasons. Therefore, the "difficulty in enforcement" has also become a common concern in the Chinese society.

Firstly, with the development of economy, China has witnessed an explosive growth in the number of civil and commercial disputes. From 2013 to 2015, Chinese courts received a total of 10,132,200 enforcement cases, while the total number of enforcement personnel in Chinese courts in the same period was only about 38,000. In courts of economically developed areas, the contradiction between "too many cases and understaffed situation" is extremely prominent.

Secondly, the condition precedent of enforcement is to track down and/or freeze the property of the party subject to enforcement. According to the Chinese law, the court will send a notice of enforcement and a property reporting order to the party subject to enforcement, requiring it to take the initiative to report its own property information. However, according to our experience, it is quite rare for the party subject to enforcement to voluntarily report its property information. Therefore, the court needs to take the initiative to track down the property of the party subject to enforcement. Because the information systems of courts, banks and government departments in charge of property information registration are not all interconnected, generally, the court staff need to go to several organizations personally to query the

---

[1] *CPL (Revised in 2021): Article 231, 243, 246, 248–251, 288–290.*
Judicial Interpretation of CPL (Revised in 2022): Article 543.
Civil Enforcement Law of the People's Republic of China (Draft published in June 2022): Article 15.
《中华人民共和国民事强制执行法(草案)》(2022年6月发布).
Report on the Enforcement Work of the People's Courts (Published in 2016), see: https://www.court.gov.cn/zixun-xiangqing-17862.html.
《人民法院执行工作报告》(2016年发布).
Report of the Supreme People's Court on Works of People's Courts to Resolve the "Difficulty in Enforcement" (Published in 2018), see: https://www.court.gov.cn/zixun-xiangqing-124841.html.
《最高人民法院关于人民法院解决"执行难"工作情况的报告》(2018年发布).

property clues of the party subject to enforcement, thus resulting in the inefficiency of enforcement to some extent.

Thirdly, since China's credit reference system still requires further improvement, the punishment against dishonest judgment debtors is insufficient. This has, to certain extent, provided a breeding ground for the party subject to enforcement to transfer its property, evade or resist enforcement, which in turn makes it more difficult to carry out the enforcement.

(Reference provisions and information for Sect. 10.2).[2]

10.3 Track Down and/or Freeze the Property of the Party Subject to Enforcement Through the Information Network System

In order to improve the efficiency in tracking down property, on 24 December 2014, the SPC, in concert with the People's Bank of China, the State Administration for Industry and Commerce, the China Banking Regulatory Commission, the China Securities Regulatory Commission and other departments, officially launched the Online Enforcement Query and Control System for courts nationwide. As of October 2018, the System has been connected with 16 units including the Ministry of Public Security, the Ministry of Civil Affairs, the Ministry of Natural Resources, the Ministry of Transport, the People's Bank of China, the China Banking and Insurance Regulatory Commission and more than 3900 banking and financial institutions, making it possible to inquire into 25 items of 16 categories of information such as real estate, deposits, financial and wealth management products, ships, vehicles and securities nationwide. By September 2018, Chinese courts have conducted property inquiries in 57.46 million cases through the Online Enforcement Query and Control System, and tracked down 5.46 million pieces of real estate information, 49.31 million vehicles, 108.5 billion shares of securities and 1.19 million ships.

In addition to inquiring into the property information, the court may also directly freeze and deduct the bank deposits of the party subject to enforcement through the Online Enforcement Query and Control System. By September 2018, Chinese courts have frozen a total of RMB 299.2 billion through the Online Enforcement Query and Control System.

It is worth mentioning that many courts have also established regional query and control systems with government departments within their jurisdictions. Although regional query and control systems only cover a smaller geographical area, the information tracked down may be more detailed than that tracked down by the Online Enforcement Query and Control System, and their property freezing function may be more powerful. For example, the courts in Shanghai can directly sequester the

---

[2] *Report on the Enforcement Work of the People's Courts (Published in 2016), see:* https://www.court.gov.cn/zixun-xiangqing-17862.html.

《人民法院执行工作报告》(2016年发布).

target real estate in Shanghai through the regional query and control system, so that the party subject to enforcement cannot handle the ownership change and mortgage registration.

It should be noted that query and control systems may vary from one to another in terms of their interconnection with other organizations, and so does the property freezing function. In practice, some work still needs to be done offline. Therefore, how to track down and/or freeze the property of the party subject to enforcement should still be subject to the decision of the court. However, we believe that with the continuous improvement of the functions of the query and control system, Chinese courts' ability to track down and/or freeze the property of the party subject to enforcement will get stronger.

(Reference provisions and information for Sect. 10.3).[3]

10.4 Dispose of the Property of the Party Subject to Enforcement Through Online Auction

With respect to bank deposits of the party subject to enforcement, generally, the Chinese court can directly transfer them to the court's special account through the query and control system, and then hand them over to the applicant. With respect to other properties (including but not limited to real estate, movable property, equity, intellectual property, and other intangible assets), generally, the Chinese court will organize an auction, and use the proceeds obtained therefrom to repay the applicant, with the balance returned to the party subject to enforcement.

In the past, judicial auctions were conducted offline. However, due to insufficient information disclosure and other reasons, there are many disadvantages in offline auction, such as time-consuming, huge amount of commission, low deal closing rate, and easy to give rise to corruption. In order to solve these problems, Chinese courts have comprehensively implemented the online judicial auction reform since 1 January 2017, and now, most of judicial auctions are conducted through the Internet.

The general process of online judicial auction is as follows:

Firstly, the court appoints professional valuation agencies to value the auction item and determine the starting price.

Secondly, the court issues an auction announcement through the auction platform and other channels provided by law in advance, discloses the auction rules and auction item information, and begins to receive the deposit paid by bidders.

---

[3] *Provisions of the Supreme People's Court on Several Issues Relating to Property Investigation in Civil Enforcement Proceedings (Revised in 2020, Fa Shi [2017] No.8): Article 1.*
《最高人民法院关于民事执行中财产调查若干问题的规定》(2020年修订，法释〔2017〕8号).

Report of the Supreme People's Court on Works of People's Courts to Resolve the "Difficulty in Enforcement" (Published in 2018), see: https://www.court.gov.cn/zixun-xiangqing-124841.html.
《最高人民法院关于人民法院解决"执行难"工作情况的报告》(2018年发布).

Thirdly, the auction starts at the time announced by the court, and the bidding period of the auction shall last at least 24 hours. If there is a bid five minutes before the end of the bidding, the bidding period shall be extended for five minutes from the last bid until there is no new bid.

Fourthly, if the auction succeeds, the buyer shall pay the difference between the auction price and the deposit paid previously to the account designated by the court within the time limit designated by the court. The court then prepares the legal documents necessary for the buyer to register the transfer of property rights and interests.

Fifthly, if the auction fails, the court shall lower the starting price (the decrease shall not exceed 20% of the first starting price) and conduct another auction on the same auction platform within 30 days.

Sixthly, if the second auction fails again, the court shall inquire about the applicant's willingness to accept the auction item to offset the debt. If the applicant refuses to accept the auction item, the court shall organize another 60-day online sale at the starting price of the second auction. If there are bids from bidders during the 60-day sale period, the sale will again be subject to the 24-hour bidding procedure under the auction rules until the deal is closed.

At present, there are seven online judicial auction platforms, among which Taobao (www.taobao.com) and JD.COM (www.jd.com) enjoy greater influence and popularity. These two platforms are also well-known e-commerce websites in China. The applicant has the right to choose the auction platform; however, if the applicant fails to do so, the court shall designate the auction platform.

After the implementation of online judicial auction, the disadvantages of offline judicial auction have been basically eliminated. As of October 2018, Chinese courts had conducted more than 747,000 online auctions, accounting for more than 80% of all judicial auctions in the same period; more than 221,000 auction items were sold through online auction, with a turnover of about RMB 503 billion and a premium rate of 66%. On 13 July 2018, the Hengnan County Primary People's Court of Hunan Province completed an online judicial auction of the toll collection right of an expressway, with the final transaction price being RMB 10.624 billion, setting a record-high transaction price of a single online judicial auction in China so far.

It should be noted that if more than one applicant requests to enforce the same property, and there is no priority claim (such as mortgage) on the property, generally, the applicant who takes property preservation measures first will be compensated from the property first. Therefore, to apply for property preservation as soon as possible is highly critical for the applicant (for property preservation, see Sect. 9.1).

(Reference provisions and information for Sect. 10.4).[4]

---

[4] *Judicial Interpretation of CPL (Revised in 2022): Article 168.*

Provisions of the Supreme People's Court on Several Issues Concerning Online Judicial Auctions (Fa Shi [2016] No.18).

《最高人民法院关于人民法院网络司法拍卖若干问题的规定》(法释〔2016〕18号).

Notice of the Supreme People's Court on the Smooth Transition between Online Judicial Auction and Online Judicial Sales (Fa Ming Chuan [2017] No.455).

10.5 Restrictions and Punishments on the Party Subject to Enforcement

If the party subject to enforcement fails to perform his/her obligations in accordance with the court enforcement notice, the Chinese court may restrict him/her from unnecessary consumption, such as traveling by air and high-speed train, spending money and accommodating in star hotels, and purchasing houses. If the party subject to enforcement is an organization, then its legal representative will be prohibited from making unnecessary consumption, but the legal representative may apply to the court for consumption with personal property for personal needs. At present, China's railways, civil aviation and hotels have been interconnected with the court query and control system. The court only needs to input the information of the person subject to restriction, the system will then automatically reject the order of the said person. As of September 2018, the Chinese courts have restricted 14.63 million person-time to travel by air and 5.22 million person-time to travel by high-speed train. In addition, the information of the party subject to enforcement whose consumption is restricted will be published on the China Enforcement Information Online (http://zxgk.court.gov.cn/) established by the SPC.

The court and other government departments may impose more severe joint punishment on "dishonest judgment debtor". The term "dishonest judgment debtor" refers to those who have the ability to satisfy the judgment but refuse to do so, and those who violate the court order, evade or resist the enforcement. In 2013, the SPC created a List of Dishonest Judgment Debtors and tried to impose joint punishments on dishonest judgment debtors. At present, the SPC has signed documents with about 60 government departments and other organizations to impose about 150 punishments on dishonest judgment debtors, such as:

(1) Restrict the aforesaid unnecessary consumption behaviors;
(2) Restrict the access to loans and credit facilities from financial institutions;
(3) Restrict the issuance of bonds and other capital operations;
(4) Restrict the participation in government procurement;
(5) Restrict the enjoyment of preferential policies on investment, taxation, import and export, etc.;
(6) Restrict the engagement in production of food, drugs, hazardous chemicals and other special industries;
(7) Restrict the qualification to being recruited as a civil servant;

《最高人民法院关于认真做好网络司法拍卖与网络司法变卖衔接工作的通知》 (法明传〔2017〕455号).
Provisions of the Supreme People's Court on Issues Concerning the Enforcement by People's Courts (for Trial Implementation) (Latest revision: 2020, Fa Shi [1998] No.15): Article 55.
《最高人民法院关于人民法院执行工作若干问题的规定(试行)》(2020年最后一次修订, 法释〔1998〕15号).
Report of the Supreme People's Court on Works of People's Courts to Resolve the "Difficulty in Enforcement" (Published in 2018), see: https://www.court.gov.cn/zixun-xiangqing-124841.html.
《最高人民法院关于人民法院解决"执行难"工作情况的报告》(2018年发布).

(8) Restrict the holding of positions such as legal representative and senior executive of a company; and
(9) Restrict leaving China.

Generally, the period for inclusion in the List of Dishonest Judgment Debtors is two years. However, in case of serious or multiple dishonest acts, this period can be extended for another one to three years. Like those who are subject to consumption restriction, the information of dishonest judgment debtors will also be published on the China Enforcement Information Online, and some regions will also publish the information of dishonest judgment debtors through newspapers, radio, outdoor billboards and other means. As of September 2018, Chinese courts have published a total of 12.11 million pieces of information about dishonest judgment debtors.

If the circumstances in which the party subject to enforcement evades or resists enforcement are serious, Chinese courts may impose detention and/or fine on the party subject to enforcement, or even hold him/her criminally responsible. With respect to natural persons, Chinese courts may detain them for no more than 15 days and impose a fine of no more than RMB 100,000; with respect to organizations, Chinese courts may impose a fine of no more than RMB 1 million. If the party subject to enforcement is held criminally responsible, he/she may be sentenced to seven years' imprisonment at most and a fine may be imposed as well. From 2016 to September 2018, Chinese courts detained a total of 380,000 person-time of dishonest judgment debtors, and found 14,647 dishonest judgment debtors guilty of the crime of refusing to enforce judgments.

(Reference provisions and information for Sect. 10.5).[5]

---

[5] *CPL (Revised in 2021): Article 114, 118.*
Criminal Law of the People's Republic of China (Latest revision: 2020): Article 313.
《中华人民共和国刑法》*(2020年最后一次修订).*
Provisions of the Supreme People's Court on Restriction of High-level Consumption of Enforcees (Revised in 2015, Fa Shi [2015] No.17): Article 1, 3.
《最高人民法院关于限制被执行人高消费及有关消费的若干规定》 *(2015年修订，法释〔2015〕17号).*
Provisions of the Supreme People's Court on Announcement of the List of Dishonest Judgment Debtors (Revised in 2017, Fa Shi [2017] No.7): Article 1, 2, 8.
《最高人民法院关于公布失信被执行人名单信息的若干规定》*(2017年修订，法释〔2017〕7号).*
Notice on Issuing the Memorandum of Cooperation on Imposing Joint Punishments against Dishonest Judgment Debtors (Fa Gai Cai Jin (2016) No.141).
《关于印发＜对失信被执行人实施联合惩戒的合作备忘录＞的通知》*(发改财金(2016)141号).*
Report of the Supreme People's Court on Works of People's Courts to Resolve the "Difficulty in Enforcement" (Published in 2018), see: https://www.court.gov.cn/zixun-xiangqing-124841.html.
《最高人民法院关于人民法院解决"执行难"工作情况的报告》*(2018年发布).*

10.6 Recognition and Enforcement of Foreign Arbitral Awards—A Bright Future Ahead

10.6.1 Proactive Practice of the New York Convention

In 1987, China acceded to the New York Convention, a main basis for Chinese courts to recognize and enforce foreign arbitral awards.

The New York Convention aims to promote the recognition and enforcement of arbitral awards worldwide. According to Article 5 of the New York Convention, the main grounds for refusing to recognize and enforce an arbitral award are that there are defects in such procedural matters as the effectiveness of the arbitration agreement, the arbitration procedure, and the composition of the arbitral tribunal; there is only one ground for refusal in terms of the substantive issue, i.e., contrary to the public policy of the requested country.

Soon after accession to the New York Convention, there were precedents that Chinese courts reviewed the substantive issues of cases and then refused to recognize and enforce foreign arbitral awards on the grounds of contrary to the public policy. However, after a long-term judicial practice, this awkward situation has been completely corrected. The SPC has repeatedly stressed its support for international commercial arbitration on different occasions. Now, Chinese courts are very cautious and prudent in demonstrating whether the recognition and enforcement of an award would be contrary to China's public policy.

10.6.2 Other Supporting Systems

In addition to accession to the New York Convention, China has also established other supporting systems to support the recognition and enforcement of foreign arbitral awards in China.

Firstly, cases concerning the recognition and enforcement of foreign arbitral awards are tried by the intermediate courts, rather than by the primary courts as in most cases. Besides, such cases shall be tried by the internal division of the court responsible for hearing foreign-related commercial cases. This system enables such cases to be tried by more professional personnel.

Secondly, refusal to recognize and enforce foreign arbitral awards requires the consent of the SPC. Specifically, if an intermediate court intends to refuse to recognize and enforce a foreign arbitral award, it shall report the case to the high court for review; if the high court agrees with the intermediate court, the high court should report the case to the SPC for review. This system has successfully prevented local courts from abusing their discretion, which further leads to refusal to recognize and enforce foreign arbitral awards by mistake.

Thirdly, while applying for recognition and enforcement of foreign arbitral awards, the parties may also apply with the court for property preservation to sequester the property of the judgment debtor in advance. This system may prevent the judgment debtor from transferring and/or hiding property.

10.6.3 Time Limit and Application Fee

The time limit for applying for recognition and enforcement of foreign arbitral awards is the same as the general limitation of application for enforcement, namely two years (very likely to be extended to three years in the future) upon expiration of the performance period specified in the award, which can be reset by the assertion of right by the right holder, or suspended under specific circumstances.

Regarding the application fee, most Chinese courts will charge CNY 400—CNY 500, which is quite affordable to the applicant. Only few courts charge fees according to the amount to be enforced and the enforcement application fee rates.

10.6.4 Practice

During the long-term judicial practice, Chinese courts have been quite cautious in refusing to recognize and enforce foreign arbitral awards. In 2019, for example, Chinese courts closed 32 cases of application for recognition and enforcement of foreign arbitral awards, with only one case being refused for recognition and enforcement on the ground of beyond the scope of the submission to arbitration. According to incomplete statistics, in 2020, there is only one foreign arbitral award being refused for recognition and enforcement by a Chinese court, and in 2021, there is none. This also fully reflects Chinese courts' attitude in supporting arbitration.

To sum up, there is a promising future for the recognition and enforcement of foreign arbitral awards in China, and foreign parties might as well give this a shot.

(Reference provisions and information for Sect. 10.6).[6]

---

[6] *CPL (Revised in 2021): Article 290.*

Judicial Interpretation of CPL (Revised in 2022): Article 545.

Notice of the Supreme People's Court on Issues Concerning the Centralized Handling of Cases of Judicial Review of Arbitration (Fa [2017] No.152).

《最高人民法院关于仲裁司法审查案件归口办理有关问题的通知》(法〔2017〕152号).

Provisions of the Supreme People's Court on Issues relating to the Reporting and Review of Cases Involving Judicial Review of Arbitration (Revised in 2021, Fa Shi [2017] No.21): Article 2.

《最高人民法院关于仲裁司法审查案件报核问题的有关规定》(2021年修订,法释〔2017〕21号).

Notice of the Supreme People's Court on the Handling of Issues Concerning Foreign-related Arbitration and Foreign Arbitration by People' Courts (Fa Fa [1995] No.18).

《最高人民法院关于人民法院处理与涉外仲裁及外国仲裁事项有关问题的通知》(法发〔1995〕18号).

Conference Summary 2022: Article 109.

Measures for the Payment of Litigation Fees: Article 14.

10.7 Recognition and Enforcement of Foreign Court Judgments—A Pathway Worth a Try

10.7.1 Bilateral Treaties or Reciprocal Relationship—Preconditions for the Recognition and Enforcement of Foreign Court Judgments

At present, China's legislature has not yet ratified any multilateral convention on the recognition and enforcement of foreign court judgments. Therefore, for a foreign court judgment to be recognized and enforced in China, it is necessary for the country making the judgment to conclude a corresponding bilateral treaty with China or have a reciprocal relationship with China (not required in the case of recognition of foreign divorce judgment).

According to incomplete statistics, China has concluded bilateral treaties on the recognition and enforcement of foreign court judgments with 35 countries, including France, Italy, Spain and Russia. For the recognition and enforcement of judgments from countries other than the foregoing 35 countries, a reciprocal relationship with China is required.

To determine the existence of a reciprocal relationship, Chinese courts have adopted the de facto reciprocity standard for a long time, that is, Chinese courts can determine the existence of a reciprocal relationship between China and a foreign country only if that foreign country has recognized and enforced a Chinese judgment previously. However, such a stringent requirement makes it impossible for the judgments of many foreign countries to be recognized and enforced in China.

10.7.2 Significant Relaxation of the Criteria for Determining a Reciprocal Relationship

However, the SPC promulgated the Conference Summary 2022, which significantly relaxed the criteria for determining a reciprocal relationship. In the event of any one of the following three situations, Chinese courts can determine the existence of a reciprocal relationship:

(1) According to the laws of the country making the judgment, Chinese judgments can be recognized and enforced by the courts of that country;

《诉讼费用交纳办法》
Civil Enforcement Law of the People's Republic of China (Draft published in June 2022): Article 15.
《中华人民共和国民事强制执行法 (草案)》(2022年6月发布).
Annual Report of the Supreme People's Court on Judicial Review of Commercial Arbitration (2019).
《最高人民法院商事仲裁司法审查年度报告 (2019)》

(2) China has reached an understanding or consensus on reciprocity with the country making the judgment; and
(3) Either the country making the judgment or China has made a commitment on reciprocity to the other party through diplomatic channels, and there is no evidence that the country making the judgment has refused to recognize and enforce a Chinese judgment on the ground of no reciprocal relationship.

In addition, the examination and determination of a reciprocal relationship are carried out on a case-by-case basis, which means that we should not infer the future determination solely based on the previous determination of reciprocal relationship by Chinese courts. However, in order to unify the determination criteria, all cases involving the determination of reciprocal relationship must be submitted to the SPC for review level by level.

At present, the Shanghai Maritime Court has established a precedent that Chinese judgments can be recognized and enforced in the United Kingdom based on the British law, and therefore, there is a reciprocal relationship between China and the United Kingdom. Moreover, China's SPC and the Supreme Court of Singapore have signed a Memorandum of Guidance (MOG) on the recognition and enforcement of money judgments in commercial cases, so that the two countries have reached a consensus on reciprocity. We believe that, in the future, Chinese courts will recognize and enforce foreign court judgments based on reciprocity in more and more cases.

10.7.3 *Other Rules Stipulated by the Conference Summary 2022*

The Conference Summary 2022, in addition to the determination of a reciprocal relationship, also provides guidance on other matters concerning the recognition and enforcement of foreign court judgments. Here are some examples:

(1) In addition to judgments in civil and commercial cases, legal documents on civil damages in criminal cases can also be recognized and enforced by Chinese courts, excluding preservation (interim measure) rulings and other legal documents concerning procedural matters;
(2) The judgment should be an effective judgment not subject to appeal, and the main basis for determining the effectiveness of the judgment is the law of the country making the judgment;
(3) If, according to the Chinese law, the court of the country making the judgment has no jurisdiction over the case, then the judgment cannot be recognized and enforced by Chinese courts;

(4) If there are damages obviously exceeding the actual loss in the judgment, the excess part cannot be recognized and enforced by Chinese courts.

Moreover, the Conference Summary 2022 also allows the parties to apply for the preservation of the property of the judgment debtor while applying for recognition and enforcement of the foreign court judgment.

It should be noted that the Conference Summary 2022 is not applicable to the recognition and enforcement of judgments in bankruptcy, intellectual property, unfair competition and monopoly cases.

Lastly, the CPL Revision Draft 2022 has absorbed some contents of the Conference Summary 2022, such as the causes of non-recognition of foreign judgments, and has supplemented more detailed rules of determining whether the country making the judgment has jurisdiction over the case. As far as we understand, this is a positive sign of making clearer rules of recognition of foreign judgments through legislation. The Judicial Interpretation of CPL, which is likely to be revised again after the CPL's revision, may also include more detailed rules in such area.

10.7.4 Practice and Future Prospects

According to incomplete statistics, a total of 26 judgments from the United States, the United Kingdom, Germany, France, Italy, Poland, Russia, Belarus, Turkey, the United Arab Emirates, Uzbekistan, Malaysia, Singapore, and South Korea have been recognized and enforced by Chinese courts. With the promulgation of the Conference Summary 2022 and the publication of CPL Revision Draft 2022, we believe that, it will be more worthwhile for foreign parties to try to have their foreign judgments to be recognized and enforced in China in the future.

(Reference provisions and information for Sect. 10.7).[7]

---

[7] *CPL (Revised in 2021): Article 288, 289.*
CPL Revision Draft 2022: Article 302, 303.
Judicial Interpretation of CPL (Revised in 2022): Article 542.
Conference Summary 2022: Article 33, 39, 41, 42, 44–46.

Open Access This chapter is licensed under the terms of the Creative Commons Attribution 4.0 International License (http://creativecommons.org/licenses/by/4.0/), which permits use, sharing, adaptation, distribution and reproduction in any medium or format, as long as you give appropriate credit to the original author(s) and the source, provide a link to the Creative Commons license and indicate if changes were made.

The images or other third party material in this chapter are included in the chapter's Creative Commons license, unless indicated otherwise in a credit line to the material. If material is not included in the chapter's Creative Commons license and your intended use is not permitted by statutory regulation or exceeds the permitted use, you will need to obtain permission directly from the copyright holder.

Chapter 11
Settlement and Mediation

Abstract Chinese courts, influenced by the concept "Harmony is the Top Priority" in Chinese culture, have always been encouraging the parties to resolve disputes by means of settlement and/or court-connected mediation. In order to prevent the other party from reneging after signing a settlement or mediation agreement, the parties need to obtain effective legal documents from the court so that they can apply with the court for enforcement where necessary. In the process of settlement and mediation, the concessions made by the parties that are unfavorable to themselves cannot be deemed as a self-admission of the parties. However, it is necessary for the parties to take certain measures to prove that these concessions are indeed made in the process of settlement and mediation. Generally, the information involved in settlement and mediation is confidential.

11.1 The Difference Between Settlement and Mediation

In China, settlement refers to the fact that the parties resolve disputes through negotiation on their own without the intervention of the court or other organizations. Since there is no need for the intervention of the court or other organizations, the parties can reach a settlement agreement in all stages of the court proceedings. However, the settlement agreement reached by the parties is not legally enforceable. If the other party breaches the settlement agreement, the non-breaching party, rather than directly applying with the court for the enforcement (for enforcement, see Chap. 10) of the settlement agreement, needs to file another lawsuit regarding the breach. The parties can still make a settlement during the enforcement procedure, and apply with the court for suspension of the enforcement procedure after reaching a settlement agreement.

Mediation, different from settlement, is generally conducted under the auspices of the court. If the mediation succeeds, the parties may request the court to issue a mediation statement, which, different from the settlement agreement, is legally enforceable. If the other party fails to perform the obligations specified in the mediation statement, the parties may directly apply with the court for enforcement without further litigation. If the parties reach a settlement agreement on their own during litigation, they may also apply with the court to issue a mediation statement.

In order to encourage the parties to and help them resolve disputes once and for all, Chinese courts can also mediate matters beyond the claims for relief and include such matters into the mediation statement. In addition, if a party not involved in the case voluntarily provides guarantee for a party to the case, the court may also include the party not involved in the case into the mediation and specify its guarantee obligation into the mediation statement.

11.2 Mediation Organized by Organizations Other Than the Court

In China, there are other organizations, in addition to the court, that may serve as a mediator. The most common mediation organizations in China are residents' committees in urban areas and villagers' committees in rural areas. There are also mediation organizations set within some chambers of commerce, industry associations and other organizations.

In recent years, due to the growing number of cases, the workload of Chinese courts is getting increasingly heavier, resulting in many cases unable to be handled in a timely manner. In order to improve the efficiency of resolution of disputes (especially minor disputes in everyday life), Chinese courts are now cooperating with the above-mentioned mediation organizations. After the plaintiff files a lawsuit with the court, Chinese courts often first hand over the case to the above-mentioned mediation organizations for mediation without going through the formal case filing procedure. If the mediation succeeds, the mediation organization will arrange both parties to sign a settlement agreement; if the mediation fails, the mediation organization will transfer the case back to the court, which will then go through the formal case filing procedure and initiate the court proceedings. The court may also, during the litigation, refer the case to a mediation organization for mediation with the consent of the parties.

The above-mentioned pre-litigation mediation period is generally 30 days. Considering the time for files transfer between the court and the mediation organization, the pre-litigation mediation period may be longer in practice. If a mediation organization is entrusted for mediation during the court proceedings, the mediation period is generally 15 days (for cases under ordinary procedure) or 7 days (for cases under summary procedure) (for ordinary procedure, see the abstract of Chap. 5; for summary procedure, see Sect. 5.6).

It should be noted that the settlement agreement signed under the auspices of the mediation organization is not legally enforceable as well. If it is necessary to make the settlement agreement legally enforceable, the parties need to jointly apply with the court within 30 days after signing the settlement agreement, and the court will then confirm the enforceability of the settlement agreement; however, the settlement agreement will not be legally enforceable if either party refuses to do so. Therefore, if you are worried that the other party would refuse to perform the settlement agreement, we advise that you insist on the court presiding over the mediation during the court proceedings and issuing a mediation statement.

11.3 Self-admission in Settlement and Mediation

According to the Chinese law, the facts admitted by the parties to reach a settlement agreement during litigation shall not be used as a basis against them in the subsequent litigation, unless otherwise specifically provided by the law or the parties agree to waive this right. This provision on self-admission is consistent with that of many countries around the world.

However, it should be noted that only the facts admitted by the parties "during litigation" for the purpose of settlement or mediation cannot be used as evidence in the subsequent litigation. But the Chinese law fails to further define the term "during litigation". Some understand "during litigation" as "in court", while others understand it as "after the court files the case". We are in the opinion that the mediation conducted by the mediation organization under entrustment by the court before the formal case filing should also fall within the period of "during litigation".

Given that the Chinese law, principledly speaking, recognizes the probative power of secret recordings (for the probative power of secret recordings, see Sect. 6.7), some dishonest parties may record the process of settlement and negotiation, and assert that the negotiation is not for the purpose of reaching a settlement "during litigation", and then further claim that the unfavorable statements made by the other party constitute a self-admission. If it is necessary to bring such dishonest practices to a halt, we advise that the parties make it clear at the beginning of the dialogue: this is a settlement negotiation, and any facts admitted in this dialogue shall not be taken as a self-admission, and the dialogue including such statement should be recorded throughout.

Although generally speaking, the facts admitted during the settlement cannot be used as evidence, the admitted facts unfavorable to either side may affect the judge's inner judgment if the settlement fails. Therefore, during the settlement negotiation, we advise that the parties leave the facts of the case behind as far as possible and discuss the settlement offer only.

11.4 Confidentiality in Settlement and Mediation

As the process of settlement and mediation often involves the parties' personal privacy, trade secrets or information that the parties are unwilling to disclose to the public, the Chinese law stipulates that: unless otherwise agreed by the parties, the mediation process and the settlement agreement reached shall not be made public;

however, for the purpose of protecting national interests, social public interests and the legitimate rights and interests of others, the court may disclose the settlement agreement to the extent it deems necessary. In practice, it is quite rare for the court to take the initiative to disclose the settlement agreement. Not only the court, but also mediation organizations are obligated to keep the mediation process and the settlement agreement confidential. In addition, the parties may also add a confidentiality clause to the settlement agreement.

The parties may blacken the confidential content or excerpt the non-confidential content of the documents submitted to the court or the other party in the process of mediation or settlement: for example, blacken the opposite party of the contract, the contract amount, sensitive terms, or excerpt the relevant parts only, etc. Of course, blackening and excerpts should be limited to a certain range, without affecting the integrity of the whole document, nor covering up the content (such as the preparation time of the document, official seal and signature affixed thereon) critical to the judgment of the authenticity of the document, so as to avoid incurring groundless doubts about the authenticity of the evidence.

(Reference provisions and information for this Chapter).[1]

Open Access This chapter is licensed under the terms of the Creative Commons Attribution 4.0 International License (http://creativecommons.org/licenses/by/4.0/), which permits use, sharing, adaptation, distribution and reproduction in any medium or format, as long as you give appropriate credit to the original author(s) and the source, provide a link to the Creative Commons license and indicate if changes were made.

The images or other third party material in this chapter are included in the chapter's Creative Commons license, unless indicated otherwise in a credit line to the material. If material is not included in the chapter's Creative Commons license and your intended use is not permitted by statutory regulation or exceeds the permitted use, you will need to obtain permission directly from the copyright holder.

---

[1] *CPL (Revised in 2021): Article 53, 96, 100, 201, 237.*
Judicial Interpretation of CPL (Revised in 2022): Article 107, 146.

People's Mediation Law of the People's Republic of China (Promulgated in 2010): Article 2, 8.
《中华人民共和国人民调解法》(2010年颁布).

Provisions of the Supreme People's Court on Several Issues concerning the Civil Mediation by People's Courts (Latest revision: 2020, Fa Shi [2004] No.12): Article 2, 7, 9.
《最高人民法院关于人民法院民事调解工作若干问题的规定》(2020年最后一次修订，法释〔2004〕12号).

Provisions of the Supreme People's Court on Several Issues Concerning the Settlement in Enforcement (Revised in 2020, Fa Shi [2018] No.3): Article 1, 2.
《最高人民法院关于执行和解若干问题的规定》(2020年修订，法释〔2018〕3号).

Provisions of the Supreme People's Court on Specially Invited Mediation by People's Court (Fa Shi [2016] No.14): Article 1, 2, 11, 27.
《最高人民法院关于人民法院特邀调解的规定》(法释〔2016〕14号).

The manufacturer's authorised representative in the EU is Springer Nature Customer Service Centre GmbH, Europaplatz 3, 69115 Heidelberg, Germany. If you have any concerns regarding our products, please contact ProductSafety@springernature.com

Printed and bound by CPI Group (UK) Ltd, Croydon, CR0 4YY

25/03/2026

02078171-0002